OF
LIFE

effortless work and happy living through self-transformation

BY

PURNACHANDER R. BIKKASANI, MD

All proceeds from the sales of this book will be donated to help disadvantaged students

Published by Best Seller Publishing®, Pasadena, CA
Best Seller Publishing® is a registered trademark
Printed in the United States of America.
ISBN 9798633136906

This publication is designed to provide accurate and authoritative information with regard to the subject matter covered. It is sold with the understanding that the publisher is not engaged in rendering legal, accounting, or other professional advice. If legal advice or other expert assistance is required, the services of a competent professional should be sought. The opinions expressed by the authors in this book are not endorsed by Best Seller Publishing® and are the sole responsibility of the author rendering the opinion.

For more information, please write:
Best Seller Publishing®
1346 Walnut Street, #205
Pasadena, CA 91106
or call 1(626) 765 9750
Toll Free: 1(844) 850-3500
Visit us online at: www.BestSellerPublishing.org

Table of Contents

INTRODUCTION..1

    A Young Farmer...1

    A Young Doctor..3

    A Western Sojourn..4

    Building, Maintaining, and Sustaining Happiness.......................6

CHAPTER 1 Happiness Today (a buildable emotion)...................11

    What is Happiness?...14

    Happiness is on a Roll in the Modern World..............................15

    The Foundation of Happiness (three origins)............................18

    Happy Hormones..24

    Can Money Buy Happiness?..28

    Are We Happier Today?...29

CHAPTER 2 The Joy of Life...31

    Tools of Happiness...32

    The Vehicle of Joy: Stages 1-5...46

CHAPTER 3 Stage 1: The Wheels of Conflict and Change.........49

    Sweet Dreams to Lifetime Shock...51

    The Inevitability of Conflict...53

    Minimizing the Damages of Conflict..57

Accepting Failure...60

Activity: Identifying Your Conflicts...64

CHAPTER 4 Stage 2: Identifying Purpose....................................67

Loving Self in 2nd Place..68

The Purpose of Life..69

Purpose of work: Who do you work for?......................................72

Loving Self in 1st Place...73

Activity: Identifying the Purpose for Yourself.............................75

CHAPTER 5 Stage 3: Setting Goals..77

Training of the Body..79

The Moral Approach to Setting Goals..80

The Framework..84

Prioritizing and Screening Goals..86

Setting Goals for Happiness...87

Activity: Setting Your Goals...88

CHAPTER 6 Stage 4: Changing Problems to Opportunities....91

A Lone Breadwinner...93

Problems VS Opportunities..93

A Snatched Seat...95

Turning Problems into Opportunities..97

The Breadwinner Gains...100

Activity: Identify Your Potential Opportunities........................101

CHAPTER 7 Stage 5: Choosing Affirmations............................103

The Debt of Gifts..105

The Necessity of Affirmations..106

Neuroplasticity and Habit Formation..107

Pillar to Post..110

A Great Day, Every Day...112

Consciousizing the Subconscious 114

Setting Up Your Affirmations..116

From Debt to Happiness...117

Activity: Choosing Your Affirmations..118

CHAPTER 8 Committing to Charity 119

An Inspirational Leader...120

We Are All Cousins..121

Humanity Shares Everything...122

The Modern World is Our Ancestral Gift 122

The Mother of All Human Progress 123

Family Estate VS Community Estate 124

The Benefits of Charity..125

Human Diversity is a Thing of Beauty...126

Legal Entitlements...127

Building a Better World 128

Activity: Focus on Your Charity 129

CHAPTER 9 Living Free and Fearless..131

Feeling Free 133

Fear of the Unknown 135

Releasing Fear...137

Consciousize Your Fears 139

Curiosity in a Cycle of Worry 140

Activity: Consciousization Journal 144

CONCLUSION..147

The Happy Bandwagon...148

Enlightenment Bites...150

An Eternal Gift to Humanity 151

ABOUT THE AUTHOR...153

Book Description 154

This book is **dedicated** to all our ancestors who struggled to survive and build a better world for us. We should revere the explorers, adventurers, scientists, and technocrats who revealed the lands, seas, and the wonder and mystery in the universe for generations to come. In the same vein, we should express a deep sense of gratitude for the reformers, revolutionaries, sociologists, philosophers, and evolutionists for their dedication and sacrifice in building a wealthier, healthier world, where peace, freedom, liberty, and the pursuit of happiness rings. We should embellish our lives with this generational gift and fulfill our moral obligation to enrich and pass it on to future generations. The proceeds from the sales of this book will do just that: help the disadvantaged students through Awareness USA 501C3 trust.

Introduction

In this book, I share the tools that have made me a happy man. I arose from poverty to richness, backwardness to sophistication, and innocence to knowledge and wisdom. I explain the habits that have transcended my fears, frustrations, and insecurities in life. The happy adventure in this book reflects knowledge and wisdom from the East and the West. The book is written with sound scientific, evolutionary, social, and emotional underpinnings of the modern world. The tools of happiness recommended here are consistent with all belief systems, faiths, and philosophies.

Over 40 years, through my medical practice experience, I have gained in-depth insights into patients' medical, financial, emotional, and psychological issues. We are never taught how to live happy in medical school, nor does any such education exist at other schools or colleges. This book fills that void. Additionally, I hope it fulfills my moral obligation to give back to society; I borrowed my knowledge and wisdom from the pool of generational gifts that belong to past generations.

A Young Farmer

I was born and raised in a small village in the interior part of Southeast India that is now called Telangana State. I was the youngest of seven children of a peasant family. Both of my parents were illiterate, but they had a small plot of land to make a living. My family always faced difficulty trying to meet living expenses. Indeed, they constantly acquired debt.

I was sent to primary school, which was very meager: one classroom and one untrained teacher. He taught first to fifth grade, all in the same class. All he taught was basic language aspects, no special subjects. So, my education at primary school was very minimal; most of the time, I helped my parents farm instead of going to school. By the time I was in fifth grade, my parents had pulled me out of school completely and put me on the farm full time.

I was a good farmer. Even at the age of 11, I was hardened by long days of physical labor, planting paddy seedlings in the cold rains during Indian monsoons. One hot summer, my younger brother and I worked hard to load and unload lots of rocks to transport on a bullock cart. While simple, farming imbued lasting patience, endurance, and made hard work a cakewalk for the rest of my life. I would have been a farmer my entire life, except my older brother became a primary teacher. He put me back into a secondary school near his job. Due to what little I studied in primary school, my education was inferior in middle school. Anything I learned in language and math was forgotten during my year working full time on the farm.

In middle school, I was average, but when I ended up in high school, my grades were really low. I never had an inspiring teacher or purpose for my education. I flunked mathematics. Due to my headmaster's graceful discretion, he added the couple of marks I needed to pass the final, and I graduated at the bottom of the class.

My brother economically supported until that time. Because my performance was poor in high school, he felt I wasn't college material. Yet, I was curious and interested to find out what college education was like. So, I asked my mother to borrow money to pay the tuition. I wouldn't have started college if it weren't for a relative who loaned us the tuition fee at the 11th hour.

Still, I didn't know how to study in the college environment. Thankfully, a roommate of mine, a senior student, was kind enough to help me. He told me, "All you have to do is just take down all the notes the lecturers tell you and then memorize them." I followed his advice and focused on memorization in science and chemistry. Even while getting a haircut, I went over the notes in my hand, which I had written on some small slips.

Honestly, I had the farmer's mentality: I worked hard. If you give a farmer any task, they will kill it. They will go after it until the work is done. I surely began as the lowest student in my class. Luckily enough, by the end of the first semester, my scores increased to an A grade, which was a great inspiration to me. I didn't know that I had so much talent, but all I needed to do was memorize. There was no play, fun, or anything else for me; I focused solely on this approach to my studies. In truth, I wasn't even that good at memorization; however, I had the doggone determination to do it so much.

A Young Doctor

At the end of that year, I applied for veterinarian medicine. Unfortunately, or very fortunately perhaps, a minister snatched my seat for his nephew. I was told that I did not have the place to continue that path anymore. Eventually, I ended up redoing the same credit clump the next year and received even better scores for going into medicine. It felt like pure luck that I would become a doctor. Until I got into it, I never thought I would end up becoming one. In those days in India, the two things that people valued most in education was becoming a doctor or engineer. So, that was the happiest moment of my life; immediately, my fortunes went up big time—financially, socially, and even in terms of social recognition. All in all, my insecurity and poverty were erased with one stroke: my admission into medicine.

A Western Sojourn

After I finished studying medicine, I went through post-grad training in India. I had some inclination to stay there; but again, my curiosity took ahold of me. I wanted to go to England, so I did. I stayed in the UK for five and a half year, furthering my education. I worked in a National Health Program. I also obtained membership in the Royal College of Physicians in England. Then, my curiosity brought me to the United States. Although I contemplated returning to India, I was driven towards New York. In the US, I trained in internal medicine. After that, I went through special training in gastroenterology. When I was finished, I started gastroenterology medical practice in Crystal River, Florida, in July 1985.

My curiosity to learn about people, lands, culture, and lifestyles in Western society never ceased. I read extensively and traveled widely in the world. I feel like my experiences in life stretch for about 10 generations, while most people experience three to four generations. My village typifies an 18th Century farming community in India with no electricity, automobiles, television, radio, or telephone. Raised in such times, after 40 years of Western sojourn, I have joined the ranks of the top 1 percentile of the world population's income and lifestyles. The unprecedented economic growth, open markets, globalization, and freedom to travel have propelled global growth and led to my meteoric raise.

Childhood Reflections

My birth date and time are unknown, but it was near the end of WWII. Around the same time, the socialist revolutions in China, Vietnam, and Cuba were rocking the world; the National Independence struggles in India, Asia, Africa, and other countries were blazing. The price of freedom and equality sent shock waves through my district and village.

Introduction

I grew up in the hotbed of the armored peasant uprising against the landlords and Razakars—the private army of the provincial Muslim King. The Razakars would attack villages, terrorize, and loot peoples' belongings. Our district was the epicenter of the revolution, and our relatives, families, and friends were the area leaders.

This evolutionary culture made an indelible impression on my young brain, as did the landlords' exploitation and repression. I grew up committed to supporting the meek and weak in society—like poor farmers, workers, women, children, and minorities. My childhood memories of women and children crying in the dusk remain fresh in my mind; the pangs of their pain were louder than the bleating goats and crowing crows.

I will never forget the cries of one woman in particular. I later learned her husband beat her up for not being in the mood for lovemaking. Men owned their wives and had the right to abuse them. In a family hierarchy, women lay at the bottom rung of the ladder.

I was fascinated by my village structure, which was based on the hierarchy of the Hindhu caste system. The highest caste, the Brahmin class, was the intellectual class; they occupied the hub of the village. The second highest class, the Kshatriya, were the rulers and warriors; none of them lived in the village. The third class, the Vaishya, was the business class. The Sudras, were the lowest class; they included the farming class, carpenters, shepherds, people who cleaned clothes, and barbers who built their homes around the hub. The Untouchables did not belong to a caste and lived in hamlets outside the village.

I lived through the shame, humility, and insecurity of childhood poverty until I became a doctor. My fears and frustrations of finding tuition and board throughout medical school developed a permanent psychological and emotional empathy for the poor, underprivileged, and unlovable people in society.

Building, Maintaining, and Sustaining Happiness

(Chapter Summaries)

I believe this book will help the reader to enjoy a happy, successful life. If you are like the majority of people who suffer and struggle in life—financially, emotionally, or psychologically—you can use this book to overcome pain and distress and build a happy life. If you are already doing well in life, tools for happiness will make you feel happier for life.

Happiness is not a fixed bank account. It needs to be refilled and reinforced continually to maintain and enhance satisfaction. We need to garnish happiness continually by utilizing the tools of happiness presented in this book and building "The Vehicle Of Joy" (which will be explained in the book) of your kind.

Chapter 1: Happiness Today

Chapter One authenticates the idea that happiness is a buildable emotion in the modern world. It details the essential elements necessary in doing so. This chapter discusses what happiness is and the origins of happiness from three distinct sources: the activities you can do to gain happiness, how you can adapt to adversity, as well as genetic happiness. It is encouraging to find out nearly 50% of happiness can be built by adopting certain attitudes, habits, and behaviors; the remaining 50%, although inherited, could be assuaged to lead a happier life. It is a matter of knowing how and going for it. I believe strong winds of happiness and human comfort are being built steadily and progressively by every generation since human evolution. If you can make a conscious choice to be happy and create a long-lasting, meaningful life, you should be able to do so.

Chapter 2: The Joy of Life

Chapter Two deals with my life story, experiences, goals, and affirmations that propelled me to financial freedom, good health, and happiness. I share insights and strategies that helped me to accomplish a stress-free life and do effortless work. I discuss how I built a successful seven-member medical group practice utilizing the following habits: goal setting and affirmations, happy relationships, delegation, communication, empathy, friendship, and fairness. This chapter also includes an overview of a life model that I've decided to call, "The Vehicle of Joy," which involves five stages of self-work (Chapter 3-7).

Chapter 3: Stage 1: The Wheels of Conflict and Change

Chapter Three has two components, focusing on the inevitability of conflict and change. Conflict among people is a ubiquitous, necessary evil for the growth and development of humanity. The second component is focused on how the universe is in constant motion and change. Life is a constant state of growth and development relative to time and space. My number one rule is to keep an open mind to amend your habits, attitudes, and outlooks with the changing times (for example, Growth Mindset).

Chapter 4: Stage 2: Identifying the Purpose of Life

The social elite and clergy pontificate about the purpose of life. Other people give up ever knowing or attaining their life's purpose. The simple truth is the meaning of life is about helping yourself or others in society. This chapter states clearly and loudly that every person doing any work in society is meeting his/her purpose of life totally and squarely. This very idea of serving the community empowers and alleviates fears, worries, and anxieties about the meaning of life.

Chapter 5: Stage 3: Setting Goals

This chapter explains the importance of goal setting for achieving success and happiness. Modern society is complex and offers unlimited opportunities, choices, and expensive lifestyles. So, goal setting becomes mandatory to sort out your dreams in order to live an enjoyable, contented life.

The most significant caveat with goal setting is realizing goals are not a block of concrete. They provide a roadmap, not a territory. So, we should realize that goal setting is fraught with vagaries, nuance, challenges, and evolving opportunities. Before setting goals, I ran from pillar to post randomly at the apparent breaks at the moment. Goal setting streamlined my choices and actions so that I could enjoy an engaging life.

Chapter 6: Stage 4: Changing Problems to Opportunities

This chapter explores seeking opportunities at the root of problems. You will find opportunities only when you seek them. View all problems as opportunities. Did you lose a job? There are hundreds more waiting in the wings. If you went through a divorce, look for a new relationship. Failures are learning experiences; hope and audacity should be a guiding beacon in life. The world is increasingly studded with abundant opportunities. You have the luxury of doing the work you love while making a decent living in the modern world. Opportunities widen by developing extensive relationships and maintaining a positive, optimistic outlook. The audacity to dream big, be creative, and maintain a great imagination will enhance your opportunities.

Chapter 7: Stage 5: Choosing Affirmations

This chapter discusses affirmations: how to set them up, practice them and the benefits of them. Affirmations are the values and beliefs that empower you to realize your goals. They boost your positivity, optimism, and audacity in life. You should reaffirm as often as possible during the day and when you confront challenges. I memorized my affirmations so they would be handy to affirm anywhere and anytime of the day. Moreover, memorization helped me to invoke them to resolve challenges on the spot when I encountered them. If you write and stick them down somewhere, they are useless when you need them. My affirmations transcended my life: helped me stand tall, speak charmingly, feel good, and stay positive. They built my attitude, habits, and behavior for life. They went viral to my wife, children, colleagues, and the community. I have included the list of affirmations that have benefitted me immensely.

Chapter 8: Committing to Charity

This chapter discusses what charity is, how human survival and progress depend on it, the power of acting together and helping each other. Helping people in need makes you feel good and happy. Both the giver and the taker enjoy the appreciation, empathy, and gratitude of giving or taking. The desire to help others is our evolutionary instinct that helped humanity to survive and progress. A person is not an island; our lives are guided by the principles of inter-dependency and mutuality. The feeling of oneness of humanity eliminates all conflicts among people and unites us for the common good. Every human gravitates to the community, even when selfish and greedy for a while. Helping others in need activates the happy chemicals in the body that make you feel good and live a meaningful life. Scientific studies have confirmed that charitable giving makes you feel good, happy, healthy, and live a long life.

Chapter 9: Living Free and Fearless

This chapter discusses why freedom and feeling free are the ultimate joy of life. It narrates the struggles and travails our ancestors endured to achieve the freedoms we enjoy today. Being free financially and emotionally is an excellent feeling. Our ancestors, Homo sapiens, struggled for centuries to get there. They have endured the brutal cold, starvation, disease, natural disasters yet marched on being the hunter-gathers to agriculture to industry to the Internet of the modern world. Life is tough for the vast majority of people at the financial, social, emotional, and psychological levels despite the availability of the abundant opportunities to live free and fearless in the modern world. This chapter discusses the steps you can take to narrow this gap to get over fears, frustrations, and embark on a free and fearless life.

This book presents the concrete steps to what I call consciousize your fears and frustrations. Developing the awareness of fears and frustrations then noting the frequency, situations, and causes of it you help you to begin to diffuse the irrational fears. Consciousization is a terrific process that can alleviate fears and worries of all sorts. The joy of freedom unleashes emotional vitality, creativity, and audacity. Everybody cherishes total fearlessness and liberty in life.

CHAPTER 1

Happiness Today
(a buildable emotion)

"THE PURPOSE OF LIFE IS TO BE HAPPY."

–Dalai Lama

People all over the world, young and old, at all stages—whether in ancient times or modern times—cherish happiness. Each generation, since human evolution, worked very hard to improve their living conditions and that of ours. Life on earth for Homo sapiens started very toughly: scavenging for food in the brutal cold. After the hunter-gatherers advanced further towards their hard work with agriculture, then gradually developing industry and technology, we now have what we call the modern world.

We produce enough food, material comforts, and provide healthcare as well as education to a vast population in the world—in developed and developing countries. Poverty, disease, starvation, and strife have decreased drastically. The open markets, trade, outsourcing, and employment, with increased instant communications, have broken most barriers of economic, social, cultural, and political nature and made the world a huge global farm village. The monarchs, dictators, and landlords have been replaced by democracies, socialism, equal rights, and mutual respect. Likewise, slavery, discrimination, and apartheid have been abolished.

My point is that the typical person today enjoys equality, fairness, freedom, and independence. People control governments and democracies. We live in a safe, secure world where we can be happy and comfortable. All the elements necessary to live a fulfilling, happy life are within our grasp. The strife, distress, and violence we see today are very much rooted in the age-old belief systems as well as regional and cultural community diversities. This is our old baggage; in the process, we'll have to get over it. The contradictions and conflicts about national interests, trade, and immigration are inevitable; still, they can and should be resolved with the collective community interests of the entire world in mind.

Today, I believe happiness is an innate gift. Our ancestors managed to secure food, shelter, and survive in the wilderness. They evolved slowly but steadily through hundreds of thousands of years to leap into farming. The agricultural revolution drastically improved the production of food grains and the human population. Consequent human settlements along the riverbanks and wealth accumulation resulted in property ownership and trade. Their lifestyles, art, and culture flourished for over 10,000 years, and then came the scientific revolution, unleashing the tremendous human potential in creating the modern world.

The scientific revolution cascaded in the discovery of steam engines, spinning mills, new modes of production, automation, and industrialization, affecting the massive wealth and material comforts for human life. It cured starvation, disease, and improved hygiene. Material progress went hand in hand with the great wakening of human thought and social developments: freedom, liberty, civil rights, ending slavery, gaining equal rights for women and workers. The French Revolution crystallized and capped many of these achievements with the ending of monarchy and total freedom for the common man, paving the way for democracy and freedom.

French Revolution

Human history is full of people who have sacrificed their lives for the sake of their communities: the explorers of the lands (Columbus), adventurers (Vikings), reformers (Nelson Mandela), revolutionaries (Karl Marx), humanitarians (Mother Theresa), and scientists have served humanity with unconditional love (Sir Isaac Newton and Albert Einstein). Likewise, freedom fighters like Mahatma Gandhi and Martin Luther King Jr., economists (Adam Smith), and lastly, the guerilla war hero like Che Guevara have all contributed to the socio-economic developments in the modern world. Science and technology continued to unmask its potential power to manifest the Internet revolution.

The Internet revolution is the most potent, peaceful revolution ever known to humanity. Its full potential is yet to manifest; we are at the very beginning of it. It is creating an entirely new world reality: it breaks all human barriers, rich or poor, city or village, national borders, culture, cuisine, political, and faith. It opened up the world markets, outsourcing, trade, commerce, and most importantly, shares the knowledge and the know-how instantaneously without spending a penny. The Internet is transcending life on earth to manifest a new, different reality.

All the knowledge and wisdom, prosperity, progress, freedom and equality, and more are our ancestral gifts. These are some of the conglomerate contributions of the unknown and well-known heroes together. We build a happy and enjoyable life on the foundations of this innate gift. No matter how rich or healthy you are, remember to express reverence to this ancestral gift. More so, learn to return this precious gift to the society with an improved version—that's our moral obligation.

What is Happiness?

Well, it could be many different things to many different people. Happiness is not easy to define because it is a subjective feeling—meaning it's not a quantifiable or measurable entity because it is felt within oneself. Happiness is just feeling good, enjoying yourself, and getting lost in the flow of things—may be reading, playing, or the labor of love, etc. Happiness comes in many different ways. It's built best on not being unhappy or stressed—or even overcoming the unhappiness and stress— and enjoying what you do. Happiness is not a single pleasure, a constant giggle, or an eternal ecstasy, but lasting inner peace and gratification. Therefore, although there might not be a clear definition of happiness, we all feel it, and we all experience it.

Just staying happy all the time is unreal; happiness and sadness are the faces of a single emotion. They sit at the polar opposites of a single emotional continuum, and they balance and trade with each other and change positions very fast. Happiness feels much sweeter coming after sad events. Yet, happiness is a choice. Not only that, I believe it is a buildable emotion. How can we build our happiness? That is the very subject of the rest of my book. Before moving forward, I want to address the distinction between pleasures and happiness.

By pleasures, I don't mean enjoying a ride at the theme park or winning the lottery. Daily pleasures are part of the entertainment and enjoyment of a fun life. Happiness is a long-lasting fulfillment in life, not simple pleasures. Happiness also evolves based on affordability, expectations, and aspirations. A panhandler is happy if somebody drops a $10 bill in their hand. If somebody is expecting to live in a luxurious home with tons of money, they will be unhappy if they don't get it. Growing lifestyles, consumerism, and higher expectations tend to raise the bar for the set-point happiness.

A history professor, Darrin M. McMahon, Ph. D., at Dartmouth College wrote an article in *Yes! Magazine.* In this article, he argued, "People before the late 17th century thought happiness was a matter of luck or virtue or divine favor. Today, we think of happiness as a right and a matter of a choice."

A new set of standards of happiness is evolving among the millennials across the world. They want to choose a career they love, but not work to make a living. Career choice is a trendy thing in the 21st Century. The United Nations has come to value the Gross National Happiness Index (a measure of happiness, safety, security, and freedom of the people), much like the Gross National Product. The modern world offers abundant opportunities to engage in a variety of specialized businesses, professions, and services. Therefore, people can afford to do whatever they love to do while making a good living and fulfilling their dreams—the glory of happiness!

Happiness is on a Roll in the Modern World

Steven Pinker, a professor in the department of psychology at Harvard University, published a book called *Enlightenment Now* (Viking Publishing, 2018). He provided evidence that the current world is wealthier, healthier, safer, and more secure than ever before. Simultaneously, conflicts, crime, violence, and homicides are down.

Happiness today includes democracy, freedom, equal rights, and civil liberties beyond the material needs in life. Today, the world is enriched to supply food, shelter, freedom, and other basic necessities across the globe.

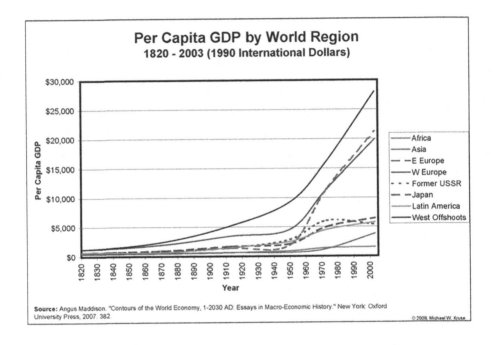

Global Economic Growth: The annual real GDP and GDP per capita have averaged 3.8% and 2.2%, respectively.

The west offshoots: United States, Canada, Australia, and New Zealand.

The above chart illustrates the global economic growth decade by decade over the past 53 years, regarding real GDP and real GDP per capita. Over the whole of the last five decades, annual real GDP growth has averaged 3.8% and 2.2% in per capita terms.

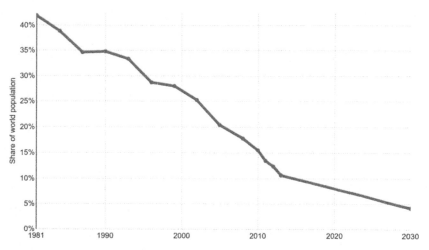

World Poverty Data

By 2015, world poverty fell 50% over 25 years. It's just about 10% in the world. By 2017, during the past 100 years, the world's wealth has gone up from $2 trillion to $280 trillion in US dollars. Life expectancy in the world today is up over 70 years, compared to about 30 to 40 years before the 19th Century.

Wealthier nations are helping underdeveloped countries. The UN Secretary-General Ban Ki-moon stated in 2015 that "The MDGs helped to lift more than one billion people out of extreme poverty, to make inroads against hunger, to enable more girls to attend school than ever before and to protect our planet." Encouraged by this success in these MDGs, the UN has chartered 17 points of Sustainable Development Goals, to be achieved by 2030.

The international institutions like the World Bank and International Monetary Fund have been providing massive infrastructure aid and help on loans for health as well as drinking water purposes. The world's non-government organizations (NGOs)—and particularly the super-rich like

Bill and Melinda Gates, Warren Buffet, and Bill Clinton—are pouring billions of dollars into sanitation, health, and drinking water. Other clubs like Rotary International, UNICEF, and countless welfare programs and religious missions are working towards making this world a better one. On this note, charitable contributions are on the rise, helping people everywhere. We are closer to a tipping point where, potentially, nobody needs any help in the future. Though it is a bit of exaggeration at this time, that day will come, in my mind.

The world is enriched with more entertainment—music, dance, drama, theater, sports (etc.)—than ever before. We can all entertain and amuse ourselves, but of course, there are still others who are worse off. I enjoy playing golf when I have nothing else to do. I do believe that enjoyable activities and entertainment decompress stress and refresh the mind so we can return to our set-point happiness. In and of themselves, they might not raise your happiness to higher levels, but they certainly recover you from somewhat low spirits or the burdens of stress.

The Foundation of Happiness (three origins)

Over time, there have been landmark discoveries about happiness. Scientists, psychologists, psychiatrists, and mental workers have been working on this issue to improve positive psychology from the start of this century. The tools that power up positive psychology could help prevent mental illness as well as boost emotional vitality and happiness. Scientists have identified three roots from which we garner our joy as discussed below.

ORiGiNS OF HAPPiNESS

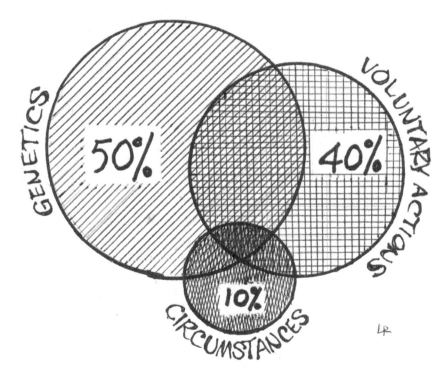

The above Venn diagram shows the origins of happiness and reflects their interrelatedness.

1. Voluntary activity 40%

2. Adapting to adversity 10%

3. Genetic (heritable happiness) 50%

The fountain of happiness springs out in three separate streams as represented in the diagram, but our happiness in daily life is the net of the total sum of these three springs at the moment. For example, the environmental factors influence heritable happiness, and heritable happiness sets a bar for set-point happiness, which in turn affects how soon a person can adapt to situational happiness. The voluntary efforts build up happiness bank accounts. Higher bank accounts override the situational happiness faster and keep us floating above the set-point happiness. One sweet spot of happiness is where voluntary activities overlap with genetic happiness. And, the sweetest area of happiness is where all three origins overlap (the smaller darkly shaded area).

Origin 1: Voluntary Activity

We should be glad to know that happiness is a buildable emotion through voluntary efforts. Sonja Lyubomirsky is a professor in the Department of Psychology at the University of California, Riverside. She's the author of the bestseller, The How of Happiness: A Scientific Approach to Getting the Life You Want. According to her, a 40% variance in our daily happiness is buildable through voluntary activities. Some activities that have fostered my happiness are: (1) building healthy relationships at home and work, (2) adapting to positive psychology, (3) draining negativity, and (4) building a stress-less life.

Building Healthy Relationships

Developing relationships is the most fundamental step in building one's happiness. A friendly or personal relationship with the boss, peers, or subordinates, is critical for earning joy. Unhappiness at work is carried home, which disturbs or distracts from family life and vice versa. We are social beings; relationships are intuitive to us and essential for our happiness. It's vital to forge positive relationships with families, friends, neighbors, peers, and communities.

Hanging out together, longing for each other, sharing joy, giving and taking, and helping each other are all part of the happy human creed. Likewise, touching, hugging, expressing love, lovemaking, empathy, and gratitude increase the happy juice in our body. Similarly, apologizing, forgiving, tolerating, and excusing make you feel good, repair relationships and help in quickly overcoming stressful situations. My success, happiness, wealth, and health are directly related to the good relationships I maintain—I'm a happy man because of them.

Adopting Positive Psychology

The benefits of positive psychology have been bought to the forefront by Dr. Barbara L. Fredrickson, a professor at the University of North Carolina at Chapel Hill. Her book, Positivity, was published in 2009. She contends that positive emotions open our hearts, minds, and perspectives. They cause us to think more broadly, seeking global differences and similarities. We also become more trusting and better at solutions and negotiations when we think positively. People experiencing positive emotions expand their field of vision and look at the background as well as the foreground, allowing us to see more possibilities creatively. For example, physicians experiencing positive emotions make better medical decisions.

There are hundreds of positive emotions: hope, amusement, interest, joy, and gratitude. Positive emotions spur our imagination, personal growth, and development. They can also utilize the negative emotions and swing us back to our set-point happiness. I encourage you to engage in every opportunity to appreciate, nurture, express empathy, gratitude, apologize, celebrate, and savor your positive emotions every chance you get. They pump each other up. I stay positive at all times. Look at the positive aspects and opportunities, even in adversities.

Amending defensive emotions:

Defensive emotions, like anxiety, worry, and fear, are necessary to prepare and fend off impending danger. It is all but natural to have these emotions when we face uncertainty or perceive risk. The body defense system invokes these emotions to boost strength and performance to protect and prevail in life. We should learn to engage these defensive emotions measured in time and scale to the situation. Excessive indulgence results in flooding the body with harmful chemicals that are detrimental to health and well-being.

Draining the Negativity: (Toxic mindset)

On the other hand, guilt, regret, revenge, jealousy, and spite are outright negative emotions that induce a toxic mindset. They are burdensome and self-destructive to the owner. These negative emotions are also much stronger, last longer, and outnumber our positive emotions. The toxic mind suffocates healthy psychological and emotional well-being. Avoiding a poisonous mindset is a priority, but if you own it already, see a counselor or talk with a trusted person—or seeking mindfulness, meditation, and yoga could be helpful.

Building a Stress-less Life

The modern world is stressful. Conquering daily stress is a stepping stone for creating happiness. Throughout this book, I share knowledge and wisdom for flying over said daily stress. For example, walking away from any given situation, counting to 100 (up or down), cooling off, and putting issues on the back burner can give immediate stress relief. Also, I always recommend meditation, yoga, mindfulness, general relaxation response, tai chi (etc.)—all of which help reduce stress. Adopting positive psychology is an antidote for a stressful life. Resolving inner or outer conflicts quickly is highly recommended (Chapter 3). Each of the chapters in this book contributes to lessen stress and to live happy.

Origin 2: Adapting to Adversity

There is abundant scientific evidence that people will very quickly get used to good, bad, and worse situations in life. Indeed, that's a good thing for us. Any of my patients who has come with dialysis, multiple sclerosis, or paralysis adapt to their inconveniences and limitations much faster than one might think. Humanity survives; that's a fact. Slaves of many civilizations survived imprisonment and torture. Some Jewish citizens and other minorities survived the labor camps, the Holocaust, and subsequently returned to their lives.

Sonja Lyubomirsky is a professor in the Department of Psychology at the University of California, Riverside; she states that contrary to many people's beliefs, circumstances like being rich or poor, healthy or unhealthy, having a disease or a disability, looking beautiful or average, or being married, single, or divorced, only account for a variance of 10% of the total possible happiness. We all gradually but inevitably adapt to our situations and get back to our set-point happiness. We adjust to good or bad circumstances in life through natural selection.

Origin 3: Inheriting Happiness

Scientific studies of identical twins have shown that happiness is genetic and heritable. No specific happy gene has been identified necessarily; other efforts are being made to find one. Something to think about is that environmental factors influence genetic factors. Professor Sonja Lyubomirsky argues in her book, "An outstanding 50% of the differences between people's happiness level can be accounted for by their genetically determined set points." However, the most recent studies estimate that variance in the expressivity of heritable levels happens to be around 33%. The inheritable happiness constitutes set-point happiness.

The set-point happiness acts by default and is the reason why people are happy or unhappy—and why they tend to remain that way for most of their lives. Set-point happiness helped our ancestors to survive the ice age, through the brutal cold, starvation, disease, and natural disasters. The happiness pumped up by activities will dissipate in time, returning our emotional state to our set-point happiness. Likewise, the events that make us feel sad and unhappy will vanquish in time, returning to the set-point happiness. Nonetheless, if we can boost fresh ounces of joy through activities, we can sustain happy moods in the longer-term.

Happy Hormones

Four important chemical molecules are produced in the brain and body that maintain pleasure, gratification, empathy, trust, and love. We're capable of creating these happy hormones by indulging in voluntary activities through exercise, expressing love, building trust and empathy, practicing gratitude, and by eating certain foods. Therefore, we can affect these happy hormones at our will; that's the reason why happiness is a matter of choice.

A. Dopamine (pleasure molecule)

Dopamine is a neurotransmitter produced in the brain responsible for propagating the signals within and between the nerve cells. The brain makes dopamine all the time from an amino acid, Tyrosine, which is present in the foods we eat. It is released during pleasurable activities, feelings of happiness, gratification, rewarding and appreciation, during foreplay, and while having sex. Dopamine also helps with sleep, mood, memory, learning, focus, and attention.

Production increases when we...

- Discover new and exciting things
- Say "awe!"
- Finish tasks

- Listen to music
- Sleep well
- Exercise
- Meditate

Foods that increase Dopamine:
- Avocados
- Almonds
- Bananas
- Green tea
- Chocolate
- Coffee
- Turmeric

B. Serotonin

Serotonin is a neurotransmitter and a hormone found in the brain and gastrointestinal tract (90%). It controls the mood and brain activity and regulates appetite, sleep, memory, learning, and sexual desire. It is widely distributed in the cerebral cortex.

Activities that increase Serotonin:

- Exercise (particularly aerobic, running, biking, and yoga)
- Sunlight
- Massage
- Remembering happy events

Foods that increase Serotonin:

- Dark chocolate
- Turmeric

- Kale
- Sweet potatoes
- Berries
- Walnuts
- Omega-3 oil
- Fish
- Red wine
- Green tea

C. Oxytocin

Oxytocin is both a neurotransmitter in the brain and a hormone produced in the pituitary gland that is responsible for childbirth and breastfeeding. Its nickname is "love hormone," and it's accountable for kisses, hugs, intimacy, trust, and social relationships. It evokes empathy, generosity, and orgasms. It is also called prejudice hormones because it favors ingrown groups over outgrown groups.

Activities that increase Oxytocin:

- Hugging
- Walking
- Laughing
- Deep breaths
- Listening to music
- Being trusted
- Charity
- Being in love
- Experiencing childbirth
- Having an orgasm

Foods that increase Oxytocin:

- Eggs
- Bananas
- Pepper

D. Endorphins

Endorphins are neurotransmitters produced in the brain. They block the pain receptors, reduce stress, and create a feeling of euphoria—similar to the experience after taking Morphine and Codeine. They improve sleep and boost self-esteem.

Activities that increase Oxytocin:

- Exercise
- Sex
- Laughter
- Massage
- Meditation
- Sniffing vanilla or lavender
- Group exercise classes
- Listening to music

Foods that increase endorphins:

- Ginseng
- Chocolate (6.7 grams a day, as in one small square 2 to 3 times a day)
- Spicy food

Can Money Buy Happiness?

Yes or no...both answers are correct.

Yes, because money is a lifeline. You need to pay for food, shelter, transportation, and work. Happiness without a home, transportation, or food is unthinkable. People without money live on the street, begging for food and shelter. The Nobel Laureate, Daniel Hahnemann, confirmed that the relationship between the family income and happiness is linear until the annual salary reaches 75,000 in American dollars. The widespread idea among people who have secured their basic needs and new age gurus think money can't buy happiness.

Andrew Blackman wrote an article titled, "Can Money Buy Happiness?" for The Wall Street Journal on November 10, 2014. He summarizes the current evidence on the question of money and happiness. He stated, "Giving money away makes people a lot happier than lavishing it on themselves. And when they do spend money on themselves, people are a lot happier when they use it for experiences like travel than for material goods." The question is: What does giving do? Helping others exudes empathy, gratitude, trust, and love for the giver and the taker. Now, we know through scientific evidence that charity boosts happiness and the immune system for a longer, healthier life. Giving migrates our emotions to our roots of humanity, interdependency, and mutuality—the love for togetherness.

Money can hurt people

The rich and super-rich could be burdened with a set of different problems. Wealthy people are vulnerable to distorted ego and estate disputes, and they forget that they stand on the shoulders of the community for their wealth and well-being. Moreover, rich people find it challenging to raise children in a way that orients them to ordinary life.

Money can't buy love, relationships, trust, loyalty, goodwill, empathy, passion, or camaraderie. It can never win a heart; however, it can corrupt minds, especially through increased access to drugs, guns, and violence. Becoming rich is certainly an adorable wish, but it could be a double-edged sword if you are not balanced in making the right choices for and with it.

Are We Happier Today?

The world seems to be in turmoil. There are so many things happening, such as conflicts with the Taliban; Al-Qaeda; ISIS; Afghan, Iraqi, and Syrian wars; nuclear threats; Arab-Israeli strife; beheadings, killings, violence, civil wars, and refugees; etc. I believe the media sensationalizes events to boost their ratings and profits. Yet, they help mount the public pressure seeking to create a better world. The historical world data indicates the world is better today than ever before, as I mentioned earlier. So, I see a different world. This was especially so once I started doing non-profit work. I'm now discovering massive charitable work is being done by countless numbers of NGOs and non-profit charities in the world (in India as well as the United States). We are building a better world for tomorrow.

Younger generations are passionate about helping others. People are helping others in need in many different ways. Social entrepreneurship is budding up, offering big scale help to people in need. The world is getting wealthier, healthier, happier, safer, and more secure by the day. Some scientists argue that life satisfaction surveys were stuck at a rate of 70% per person for a long time. This argument is weak for many reasons. The perspective and expectations of happiness are a moving target much like anything else in changing society. The availability of goods and services, affordability, and evolving lifestyle expectations impair life satisfaction surveys severely.

We measure different things in different periods. And, an unhappy person who cannot afford to buy more luxuries is not the same as someone unhappy with starvation. Satisfaction surveys are not measuring real need-based emotions, nor do they measure the effect of the adaptation factors on happiness. Therefore, life satisfaction surveys are incredibly undependable. Basically, in conclusion, the worldwide community is better off today than ever before. In my mind, after my experiences and studies, happiness is a buildable emotion.

CHAPTER 2

The Joy of Life

The joy of life has become the holy grail of the modern age. Our hunter-gatherer ancestors were barely able to survive. Yet, generation after generation has struggled and developed smarter ways of hunting and gathering, domesticating animals and plants. They developed food supplies, turned nomadic life to settlements on the riverbanks, built ancient civilizations, increased their prosperity, and improved their lifestyles. People never rested on their laurels; they perused the science and technology to enter into the industrial revolution and eventually land in the internet revolution. Every generation has been striving to build a happy, comfortable life. Indeed, the current world offers all things to all people on the planet earth to live a happy and stress-less life.

Today, the happy life is here and now. Bobby McFerrin's song, "Don't worry. Be happy" surmises the mood and mindset of people in the modern world. The material conditions for making life happy are embellished with abundant literature, books, journals, and articles advising people how to live happy, emotionally and psychologically. Here, I present the abiding resources, evidence, and tools of happiness that have worked for me. The joy I am talking about isn't egocentric or external, but a deep satisfaction with a meaningful life.

In June of 1985, I settled down in Crystal River, Florida. I started my gastroenterology practice by myself. I was determined to build a great medical practice although I didn't know how to do it. I used every possible personal relationship technique with doctors, patients, and within the community. Within two years, my practice grew in leaps and bounds; however, I was having a very tough time coping with my time balance. I found myself struggling with taking care of patients because the area had two hospitals, which were 25 miles apart. I needed to go to both emergency rooms while attending both offices and taking care of endoscopy procedures. During the peak days of my week, I worked at least 16-18 hours a day.

While so busy, I somehow managed to take a family vacation with my wife and our child. We went to Breckenridge, where I started skiing for the first time, which was great fun. Breckenridge was a lovely community, and I was on the slopes until the evening. When I returned to our room, I admired the view through the window while sipping a cup of coffee and having some chips. Whenever I could see other skiers, I watched them flying down the hills like birds without wings. It all seemed so effortless for them. Overall, it was such beautiful scenery.

At that time, I wondered, *What am I doing? Why am I so busy? I'm working so hard.* While looking into my life, I was reading a book that featured a quote from the Chinese philosopher Confucius: "If you love your work, you never work a day." That hit my heart and soul. This sentiment is something that I believe to this day. In those hectic times, I reflected very much during this guiding trip. I rapidly had some ideas about the best way to do my work. *Can this be easy and enjoyable?* As far as I was concerned, it seemed logical to me that I wasn't enjoying my work; if I was always under stress and fear, then I couldn't perform very well.

Tools of Happiness

Before I went on a skiing trip to Breckenridge, I lacked direction. I was confused. I was barely able to think through what I could do, and I hardly had any time to think of my next step. It felt like running from pillar to post, always running around headless. I was aimless without any specific activity. Due to my realizations at Breckenridge, I was able to set up goals and affirmations in my practice. Below, I list the other tools that have helped me to work happily and stress-less for the next 30 years.

1. Setting up goals and affirmations
2. Hiring the right help on time
3. Delegating
4. Building teamwork
5. Communicating (my forte)
6. Doing stress-less work
7. Doing effortless work
8. Birthing a stress management program
9. Conducting public seminars and workshops
10. Starting nonprofit work

1. Setting up goals and affirmations:

Following the vacation trip to Breckenridge, I started setting up goals for my personal life and my medical practice for the first time in my life. I had set short-term, long-term, and lifetime goals. Likewise, I selected a list of inspirational and empowering affirmations. Once I memorized the affirmations, they were handy to reaffirm any time of the day and anywhere; also, I could find rapid solutions to tough challenges by invoking the affirmations at any moment. Affirmations helped me think through how to handle, simplify, and resolve my obstacles. One way or another, win-win or compromise, these were powerful resources.

My goals were mostly about my personal life: reading, exercising, scheduling patients, expanding the practice, and building endoscopy centers whereas my affirmations were about reaffirming my beliefs and values. For example, I made a point of saying that I feel great to my patients and colleagues, or I told them to have a great day. This word is beautiful for me. Even now, each time I say "great," my body erects itself, straight and up, and my neck extends as I am filled with pride. Indeed, that phrase became so popular that my employees started to use it themselves, as did my family and friends. I share more about affirmations in Chapter 7. Nonetheless, this type of inspiration was excellent.

My goals, and particularly my affirmations, became a large part of everything I did. I discovered that I was able to solve issues much faster. The Confucius quote about work that previously inspired me cascaded deeper meaning of service and love of labor as well as purpose in my life. I was determined to be happy at work, no matter what. I challenged myself to somehow ease up every problematic or stressful situation.

2. Hiring the right help on time

One successful strategy for my medical practice was to recruit fresh graduates from medical school and nursing staff ahead of our needs, which pushed our medical practice to grow faster. I found new associates every second or third year until I had six doctors; we never had a shortage of workforce. Likewise, we recruited employees as needed. Although I'm very cautious about overhead, I recruited whenever necessary. The idea is if you plan big, you can grow big. Many medical practitioners fear expansion, so they remain solo. I believe hiring help on time is key to growing and flourishing in business.

3. Delegation

We not only hired new doctors on time, but delegated management responsibilities based on their strengths. I assigned administrative and management duties to the young associates and guided them in doing so, which was a big help because it saved much of my time to market and grow the medical practice. Most senior doctors fear to let the recruits take the responsibilities for fear of losing the power or not trusting their strengths. Delegation imbues trust and cooperation among the associates. Each physician in charge of certain parts of the practice, (the endoscopy lab, office, etc.) made management decisions through consultation and consensus with other physicians in the group. Otherwise, all management decisions were decentralized and democratized. We worked as a family, so every decision in practice was made with unanimous consent for 30 years.

Moreover, I believed empowering the associates and employees with full trust and encouragement, which helped them to enjoy their work and grow. Because of the camaraderie and friendship, we were able to accomplish much together. All the physicians and staff were pleased; consequently, everybody gained monetarily and emotionally. We believed in splitting the "big cake" equally (a great example of win-win) as opposed to everyone fighting for a larger slice.

I was fortunate enough to receive relief from my associates from being on call for emergencies, sell my practice upon retirement, leave my patients in the able hands of the associates, and, most importantly, I left the practice with goodwill and friendship. I believe leaders should be capable of trusting and delegating work to nourish people below them in the network.

4. Building teamwork

To build teamwork within our group practice, I made a point to have meetings with the staff to discuss the spirit of service. "Whom are we working with? What is our purpose?" I talked with employees again and again until they came to understand the value of compassionate, topnotch medical care to our patients. They understood that the patient is their boss, not me; the patient helped to pay their salaries. The result was a great team spirit surrounding the purpose of their work: the patient first. I reminded the employees at the right moment that patient care is all that matters. All the employees were familiar with the administrative policy that mistakes are learning experiences; we talked about it and did it right the next time. Such open-mindedness and transparency helped us build great teamwork with the employees.

I took a personal interest in helping employees with health care or financial emergencies. Some of them were single mothers, barely making enough to get by on a monthly budget. If their A/C at home or the old clunker broke, they didn't have savings to replace or repair them. So, I loaned them money without interest to be paid back at their affordable pace.

I set a mission statement for the medical office to treat all patients the same way, whether they were Medicare or Medicaid, had money or no money, or had well-paying insurance or not. We saw and helped all patients; the word spread around the county. We guaranteed patient satisfaction; I paid back the consultation fee if the patient wasn't satisfied or misinformed. The employees developed a great spirit of service according to the mission and policies of the group practice. If you ask any Publix employees for help, they walk you to the aisle where you can pick the stuff you want. My competitors were cherry-picking the best-paying patients as solo practitioners while my practice grew to a seven-member group practice —all because of our patient-centered policies.

5. Communicating (my forte)

I considered myself the king of communication, even with the toughest patients; indeed, I accepted to see such patients within my group. In my mind, the art of conversation came down to listening patiently to figure out precisely what was on the patients' minds before I spoke to them. Once the patients' concerns were alleviated, they were ready to listen and learn from us. Listening with an empty mind without thinking or preparing to answer helps us to understand the speaker. Listening with empathy, regard, and respect builds trust for a heart to heart communication. Miscommunication results from each party wanting to "upload" their mind first—which I refer to as "Me first."

The conversation is productive when spoken clearly, precisely at the level of the patient's comprehension. The speaker should know that people come to understand at different levels of vocabulary, speed, volume, and tone that match with listeners' skills. When I finished talking to patients, I asked them if they understood. When in doubt, I asked them to tell me what they understood. If they didn't get it, I summarized the meaning in a sentence or two and asked them to repeat after me or write it down in a line or two.

6. Doing stress-less work

This book is for anyone who fears, is frustrated by, and hates going to his or her daily job. It's for people in conflict with management and colleagues about their salaries, benefits, discrimination, or mistreatment at work. "If you love your work, you don't have to work a day in your life." This quote from a Chinese philosopher reverberates in my mind and heart eternally. Either find the work you love or learn to love the work you do. Look at the scores of musicians, painters, singers, and artists who enjoy their hobby. You should match their dedication and joy in your profession. There is a distinct social change I noted while working with high school students in India and the US: they are going after the jobs they love to do.

The following five steps can help relieve stress at work.

1. Realizing the purpose of life.

Alleviating the fears, frustrations, and conflicts at work begin with understanding the purpose of your work. You should know, no matter what job you do for pay or charity, you are not just making your living but serving humanity. Your status, pay, power, rank, or gender has no bearing on that purpose. A janitor in the White House or the President of the USA fulfills the same purpose of helping others. The spirit of service fosters dedication and commitment to enjoy work. Yet, disputes at work in protecting our self-interests are inevitable. So, viewing the conflicts in light of this service will help us resolve them much easier and in a less painful manner.

2. Peace of mind and tranquility.

Stress-less work is only possible with mental peace and tranquility. You can attain peace of mind by building "The Vehicle of Joy," as discussed in Chapters 3 - 7 of this book.

A. Resolve inner conflicts: Aligning the emotional and rational minds help to make conscientious choices with a peace of mind. The indecisiveness, confusion, and internal struggle to say "Yes" or "No" to "Do" or "Not" disable the body and mind. They are often the source of stress. Synchronized thinking, feeling, and doing eliminate the inner conflict.

B. Resolve the external conflicts smartly. These are conflicts between your self-interests and that of the outside world. The evolving conflicts can be anticipated, prevented, or managed to take a path of least resistance. Some well-known strategies are win-win, compromise, and give and take; they can save us from losses and stress.

C. Temporizing the stress. Prevalent practices such as yoga, meditation, mindfulness, tai chi, and general relaxation response help reduce stress and create peace of mind. Any measure that calms the mind, relaxes the body, cools off the amygdala (the emotional troublemaker), lessens the mental clutter, boosts the immunity, and resurrects the sanity is beneficial. These stress reduction techniques need to be practiced regularly to sustain long-term benefits. The tools I recommend in this book will reorient your attitudes, habits, and behavior for life. But we need to practice these tools long enough (typically a year) to hardwire our brain through neuroplasticity.

3. Adopt a calm, collected demeanor at work or home.

My rule was to stay calm and collected at work, no matter how busy I was. I could be in a great hurry and moving fast, yet, I remained calm and collected. I went after tougher challenges with a greater calm and sharper mind to work creatively to perform efficiently. This demeanor keeps our emotional hijacker, amygdala, in check and holds it to the right balance between the emotion and the reason. A calmer mind exercises creative, rational thoughts to make balanced choices between self-interests with mutual interests and less likely to get you in conflicts and frustrations. As a doctor, I realized patients don't like doctors who rush and hush. Even when I had only a couple of minutes to spare, patients felt I had all the time on Earth for them. I visited them later if I needed to, instead of rushing.

4. Enjoy hard work or easy work.

I learned to enjoy an adrenaline rush with hard, urgent work and leisurely work. I believe that nobody "dies" of hard work; the suffering is often mental conflict in deciding and dedicating to the cause. If a mind is clear and happy, the body can endure any hard work. The ability to vary the pace according to priorities at work would get me through the day happily. The clarity in thought, purpose, making choices, committing, and keeping the end in mind can deflate much of the daily stress. I cringe when a teacher or parent asks a student or child, "Are you tired?" The word "tired" is most disabling, and it should be discarded from the vocabulary. The word exhaustion can do in its place.

7. Doing effortless work

This type of work is working with the least possible physical effort without fatigue or mental stress. It is a choice one can make. The effort, in and of itself, isn't the cause of emotional or physical stress; it's our state of mind. The mind and body are two facets of a single physiological entity. Therefore, the mental stress and physical distress run in tandem, one affecting the other for better or worse. The culprit here is the mind, not the body. Poor body posture at work, at sport, or in life leads to exhaustion and mental stress. Take advantage of the body's antigravity mechanics at work to avoid fatigue, pain, stiffness, and occupational disabilities or diseases.

The critical concepts of the effortless work:

A. Antigravity posture

It's taken a million-plus years for the human race to stand up and walk—to establish the supremacy over the animal kingdom—which is great human strength. We should use it to the extreme of a good degree, holding the anti-gravity posture at work. Basically, standing tall and relaxed and maintaining normal lumbar lordotic spine curvature while sitting for long hours can help us prevent many musculoskeletal ailments. Watch people in the streets, airports, and rail stations we see all types of awkward body postures, bending forward or backward or sideways, shoulders dropping, leaning the head on one side—they squander the mechanical advantages of the antigravity posture. What is worse, they are not aware.

The antigravity posture requires that your ears sit over the shoulder, shoulders over the hips, the hips over the knees, and the knees over the ankles in a straight line. The head weighs about 10 pounds; if it sits over the shoulders, you can avoid pain stiffness, arthritis, and disc problems in the neck. I talk and demonstrate correct body posture in my motivational talks to students regularly. Unfortunately, most occupations require a compromised position at work; worse still, people are unaware of their posture until some medical issue surfaces.

B. Mechanics of antigravity

The human body has 206 bones and 650 muscles that help us stand, balance, and walk. There are four symmetrical pairs of weight-bearing joints: shoulder, hip, knee, and ankle joints aligned in a straight-line on either side of the body. The body posture is a dynamic that requires almost every bone and muscle tensing and relaxing reciprocally, making subtle adjustments with any change of posture and movement. Two more organ systems: cerebellum and proprioception (deeper pressure sensory systems in the muscles, ligaments, and tendons) play critical roles in maintaining our balance and posture.

C. Developing body awareness

Typically, we don't pay attention to our posture while walking or working, more so when we are immersed at work. We do it automatically. Body awareness requires conscious effort to check your body posture periodically and correct it promptly. Proper body mechanics help us work with ease and less trauma to the body.

For example, in my profession, gastroenterology, I have to stand long hours, staying still while doing the procedures. We need to lean, twist, and turn—hours and hours of work in those positions. My mind is fully occupied looking for ulcers, polyps, and cancers while focusing on one spot at a time. While the body and mind are focused intensely, I am unaware of my body posture and distress. As a result, the muscles, joints, and ligaments get stiff and painful. In the long term, it causes chronic aches and pains, arthritis and stiff neck, back pains, and neck pains, etc. I know many doctors who suffer from such occupational disease and disabilities – all for not watching their anti-gravity posture at work.

Different occupations adapt to different postures: people working on computers, driving trucks, or sitting for hours lose normal lumbar lordships, overuse fingers, and have stationary legs, which predisposes them to several medical ailments. We must be aware of our posture at all times and take corrective measures to stay anti-gravity to avoid the onslaught on our body and mind. The body posture is also habit prone, so the individual is unaware of poor posture. Just noticing your bad posture occasionally doesn't do any good; a sustained conscious effort for several weeks is necessary to correct bad posture.

D. Mind commands body obeys

The mind can command any part of the body to relax; this is the principle in yoga, progressive relaxation, mindfulness, general relaxation responses, tai chi, and exercise, (etc.) I keep a constant watch on my posture as well as developing tension, aches, and pains in my body. I act immediately to diffuse anything by changing posture, shaking or stretching, doing a mini massage, or taking a momentary break. Knowing what I know now, I stand tall, relaxed, grip the endoscope lightly, take deep breaths, and change posture, etc. If you can detect distress, you can fix it. I was able to avoid the brunt of physical stress on the body during my medical practice, and it has become my lifestyle. Easy work feeds mental clarity and efficiency.

I made a point to hold the endoscope softly to avoid tension and fatigue in the hands. The limiting factor here isn't shaking the distress away; it's not sensing and registering bad body posture and pain while fully immersed in doing the work.

Occupational issues are big in the workplace. Adapting to the right posture, changing posture when needed, avoiding overuse, and employing the correct ergonomics can save us billions of dollars—aside from preventing disabilities and disease. If you are pumping gas, hold the nozzle a little lighter instead of holding it tight. If you are chewing food, do it gently; fast and hard chewing grates your teeth.

The concept of effortless work can be applied to everything you do in life. Just relaxing the body while working is immensely gratifying. The time to relax is when you feel the most stressed or distressed, and the relief is immediate. All you need to do is think about it and make it a habit to relax while standing, walking, talking, playing (golf), or driving your car. If you can think about it, you can do it until it becomes a habit for you. Relaxation is a passive mental exercise; if you learned to relax at work, you could prevent many occupational illnesses.

8. Birthing a stress management program

Early in my medical practice, I noticed a third of my patients had recurrent symptoms not curable with drugs. They were complaining of symptoms related to stress, which was particularly common among women and young girls. I discovered their problems were not necessarily medical but often referred to as socioeconomic reasons—or conflicts with family, faith, beliefs, or attitudes.

I would speak with them 1-on-1 until I tired and felt that I couldn't do that kind of counseling regularly. First of all, it took a lot of time. Secondly, I was doing the same boring talk every time, every day, with many patients, which wasn't effective. Just talking doesn't pay doctors; our job is doing procedures and other related things. Teaching and training others how to live stress-less helped me to live that way. Everything I advise is well formulated in my mind, and I practice what I preach.

Though it wasn't efficient to do individual counseling, I continued wherever it was necessary. I began developing group counseling, and I started in my medical office lobby in the evening at 5 pm. A group of my patients would come, and I would help them learn stress management. Some wanted me to provide prescriptions; unfortunately, most of the pills that people do are tranquilizers, which makes their stress even worse. In too many cases, I found that if patients were referred to health counselors, psychiatrists, or psychologists, they wouldn't go due to the taboos attached to the idea.

9. Conducting public seminar and workshops

After I implemented group counseling, within a month of sessions, we could not accommodate everybody. We decided that we would go out and start public seminars and workshops. I did this for several years in the community, and I worked with a variety of groups: workforces and organizations, women, children, and families. Through this outreach, we were able to help people understand life management and working towards a stress-less life. I enjoyed it immensely at the time.

During the development of the above seminars and workshops, I also wrote articles in the local newspapers; they were published in the *Tampa Bay Times* and the *Citrus Chronicle*. I wrote several on attitude, the purpose of life, how to communicate well, how to set and practice goals, and affirmations. I compiled all the articles into a booklet called, "Blissful Life: A Way to Reach," and I would give it to my patients. It helped them to read and understand it for themselves; when I spoke with them individually, they were able to follow a lot faster. This program had a tremendous influence on my office staff, associates, and patients.

10. Starting non-profit work

Awareness USA: A few years before I planned to retire from active medical practice, I sharpened my skills in writing and speaking in public by attending Toastmasters Club and the like. I pondered what type of public service would make the most social contribution. I decided to go after education and helping the underprivileged students in India and the USA.

I retired from active medical practice in 2015 when I felt financially free. I committed to doing charitable work for the rest of my life, along with other interests: reading, writing, being an entrepreneur, enjoying family, playing golf, and enjoying life. Up to that point, I never liked the word retirement. When my patients asked me, "Doc, when are you going to retire?" I would say, "I'll retire when I am in the grave, and not a moment before." Indeed, people who retire age faster and lose interest in life. I wanted to focus the rest of my life on enjoying things I like and helping others.

After four or five years of soul searching, I founded a trust by the name of Awareness USA, which is a tax-free status 501(c) in the United States. The goal is helping deserving students and youth, particularly in underserved neighborhoods, in one form or another. We provide financial aid and assist the underprivileged students in realizing the American dream. We help with school supplies, tutoring, motivating, and counseling until they attend a degree course. We motivate them to become responsible citizens socially and to say no to drugs, alcohol, guns, and violence.

Chaitanya Saradhi Trust in India, 80G (Tax-free): I also formed another trust in India. Of course, I felt obliged to America because I owe my life to the US and am now an American citizen, but I still had a love for my mother country where I was born and raised. As I used many of their resources to get where I am today, I found Chaitanya Saradhi in

India. Through that program, I started computer education classes in the government schools where there were none. That program is going very well today.

I visit India at least two or three times a year. For two weeks, I visit school after school, giving talks, inspiring students, and inspiring teachers. Indeed, this time is the happiest of my life. These two trusts are my long-term commitment. It's what I've been doing, and it's what I want to do.

The Vehicle of Joy: Stages 1-5

Now that I've established more of my efforts in building happiness for myself, my patients, and my practice, I want to share the five stages of my book, which will help you build your Vehicle of Joy.

The Vehicle of Joy is a mental exercise where you build your dream car, putting together the essential elements of happiness discussed in this book. This "do it yourself" training imparts the knowledge, relative roles, and relationships of each of the core habits of happiness to you. The four wheels deal with conflict and change; time and space whereas the purpose of life connects all the wheels to the transmission to lay the foundation for the vehicle. The engine (affirmations), body (goals), and steering (opportunities) are the tools at your disposal to build a beautiful car of your choice. Besides, mind-mapping helps in checking and troubleshooting the mechanical problems of the Vehicle of Joy since the tool kit of happiness elements is handy at your mind's eye.

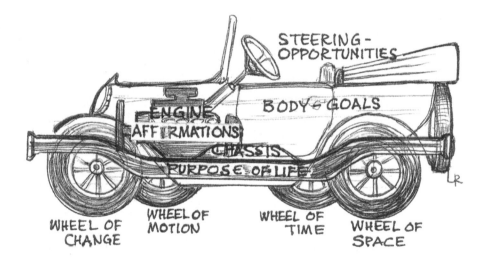

Each stage of the Vehicle of Joy is covered individually in Chapters 3 through 7, and each one leads to a better understanding of and action with the next. I hope this approach will bring much depth, clarity, priority, and hierarchy.

You should be who you are. You should live the way you want to live. Now that I have shared the Vehicle of Joy, we will launch into the stages of building happiness. The next chapter focuses on the inevitability of conflict and change.

CHAPTER 3
Stage 1: The Wheels of Conflict and Change

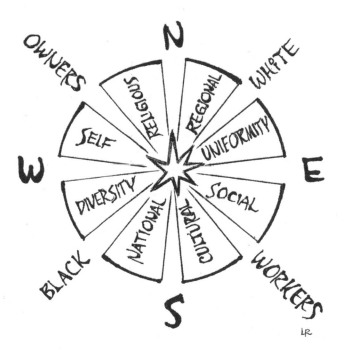

The above diagram depicts a global view of polarity, duality, diversity, contradictions, and conflicts in a society. In this chapter, you will learn why struggles are inevitable, and how their early detection, prevention, or resolution is critical to living stress-less and happy.

Conflict is a clash or friction between opposing sides regarding ideas, people, systems, attitudes, and behaviors. As we all know, conflict is worrisome, stressful, and harmful to all parties involved, and it isn't totally avoidable. Conflicts instill emotional damage, fear, anxiety, and frustration. Sometimes, it goes to the extremes of revenge, violence, and death. Overall, it affects our relationships; it's very tough to be happy when you are in conflict—whether at home or anywhere else.

Conflict is inevitable because the world is made up of opposites: north and south, east and west, positive and negative, women and men, Yin and Yang, etc. The entire universe, from subatomic particles to planets and entire galaxies and star systems—including the living and non-living—is a conglomerate of forces that keep motion and energy going between opposites. Therefore, by the very nature of this reality, conflict is inevitable.

Simultaneously, conflict is a contributing factor to growth and development. Every achievement anybody accomplishes usually follows a conflict—much like the movements for equal rights, civil rights, voting rights, workers' rights, etc. Social progress is a reflection of some form of struggle and some type of justice. Therefore, conflict contributes to growth and development.

Knowing that conflicts are unavoidable and a necessary evil, we should be smart enough to anticipate, preempt, or solve them quickly and smoothly in order to enjoy the ride in the Vehicle of Joy. The wheel of change is one among the four wheels of the Vehicle of Joy. It is entirely our responsibility to spin and service the wheel of conflict in pace with the wheel of time, space, and change. If and when the wheel of joy gets bogged down in a conflict, it derails all other wheels from doing their job towards building happiness.

This world is ever-changing, and conflict accelerates and drives the change. People, cultures, socioeconomic conditions, beliefs, and attitudes change with time. Economic growth, reforms, revolutions, technological advances, and expectations orchestrate the changes in our lifestyles, attitudes, and habits; in contrast, human instincts tend to stay put, out of the fear of uncertainty. Adjusting to a new boss, new rule, new direction, or downsizing evokes fears (real or perceived) and frustrations, so we resist the change.

The wheel of change is the second of the four wheels on which the Vehicle of Joy cruises. The wheel of change needs to spin in tune with the racing wheels of time and space. It is our job to figure out the right thing to do and the right time to surf on top of the cusp of change, which means discarding old habits, attitudes, and behaviors for new ones that fit with the changes, times, and circumstances. I can't overemphasize the need for change, just by making changes in your attitudes and habits you can get over most of your fears, frustrations, and stress. When the wheel of change is stuck, the Vehicle of Joy comes to a screeching halt, drowning us in stress and unhappiness.

How do you do the right things at the right time? That's a key question. Knowing that we have to change isn't enough; making the right change on time is where people are lost in regard to opportunities. I tumbled many times and found myself beaten before I learned how to change on time. It's possible to change too fast, too soon, or too late. I felt that learning to change was like learning how to skate. I believe opposing opinions, versions, and arguments are all correct, but they are correct in a different time and space. Instead of saying what someone said is wrong, I tell them what they say is relevant to a different time and situation.

Sweet Dreams to Lifetime Shock

I married my childhood sweetheart, Aruna. She was educated in the same high school and attended medical school a couple of years behind me. Our marriage was a fairytale because we came from small adjacent villages in the most interior parts of India. There was not much education available at that time. We were the only people who went to medical school on merit from our area. We both had common friends and families; our community was very close. Interestingly, her father was a leader who fought for the rights of poor peasants and laborers against the landlords and local government. In that way, he was my hero and had my loyalty.

I started medical school in 1965 while Aruna arrived a few years later. In medical school, we hung around the same friendly circles. I also visited her frequently because I knew her for such a long time. For some reason, perhaps because of my seniority at school, I felt I was her advisor. Whether she felt she needed my advice or not, I couldn't tell, but we were friendly and got along very well. Our friendship grew, and we fell in love. I proposed to her, and upon her consent, we married in early 1973.

The marriage went very well, and it was very simple. We were extremely ambitious, hardworking, intelligent, successful people. We did post-graduation training in India and had a baby to raise. A few years later, we moved to England to do the same: further training, further job opportunities, and continuing to raise our son. So, we were very, very busy in England, and several years of our lives passed in this way.

One day, Aruna told me that she was very distraught and had been contemplating separation and even divorce. It was a total shock to me. I was very apprehensive about a divorce; we had a child and outstanding bonds, her father was my hero, our families had grown together, and we were generally involved with the same social circles. Up to this point, I thought she and I had a strong bond as well.

I asked her what her reasoning was: What was bothering her? What was the problem? She told me that I was dominating every conversation, and I was not valuing her opinions. She felt suffocated for several years before she ever brought it to my attention. I had no option other than changing. So, I promised I would do so.

We patched up our differences and moved to the United States. For the first few years, we were once again busy with further education, training, raising our son, and settling in a new foreign country. Life went on that way, and then we moved to Crystal River, Florida, to practice medicine. While I focused on my Gastroenterologist career, she focused on hers as a Radiologist. We were both extremely successful and considered top-notch doctors in the community.

Everything went well. We settled in the new area and built a home, but something was missing. There was no intimacy or love, and there remained, to some degree, a slow sense of separation. I would sit on a sofa while she sat in a separate chair. We were living like roommates, which was pretty bothersome. We talked about it. While there was no overt conflict, she was emotionally detached from me.

We realized there was a problem with our marriage, so we decided to see a marriage counselor. It didn't help. Then, the question of divorce came. However, we needed to consider problems beyond our relationships. Namely, her younger sister was unmarried. In India, the news of an older sister's divorce affected the prospects of the younger sister getting married. Also, our son was in his final year of medical school. So, we decided to wait.

The Inevitability of Conflict

Conflict is ubiquitous and a double-edged sword. It helps if you deal with it properly. Disputes can be damning emotionally, psychologically, and socially; they might ruin your entire happy life. Conflict led to the deaths of 20 million people in WWII. Even now, there is a wide range of conflicts in the world, such as the Israeli-Arab conflict. There have always been, always are, and always will be conflicts. Right now (2018), the US government is shut down due to the battle between Republicans and Democrats regarding the construction of a wall along the southern border.

For the purposes of this chapter, I will explore two types of conflicts:

1. Inner conflicts
2. Outer conflicts

Conflicts of the mind are the worst that I have struggled with, even during the creation of this book. Inner conflict is a battle of two brains within each of us: (1) the rational brain that we normally call the cortical brain or prefrontal cortex, and (2) the rest of the lower parts of the brain that controls the subconscious behavior. The inner conflict is between "to do" or "not to do," and what is right and what is wrong. It's a struggle between conscience and instincts and between reason and emotion.

The Duality of the Human Mind: Conscious VS Subconscious

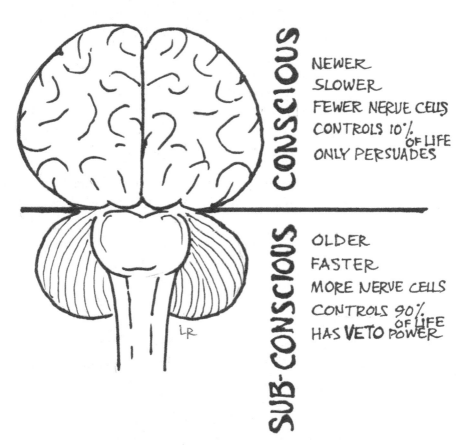

The picture above reflects two sides of human behavior: conscious and subconscious. The understanding of the relative significance of anatomy, physiology, and their role in our daily behavior in life is discussed below.

The human brain is a mystery. The mind and brain, and their relationship, remain in the dark, even to neuroscientists. A host of new technologies: PET scans, CAT scans, EEGs, etc., are used to attempt to make inroads in exploring the final frontier, the human brain. I believe the Homo sapiens' brain is about 10% humanized, and the rest is reeling in subconsciousness. I expect we will fully refine ourselves in bits and pieces through consciousization (discussed in the chapter on affirmations). Or perhaps, we will take another evolutionary leap forward to humanize fully.

For now, we live by our attitudes, habits, preferences, and motivations that are controlled by our subconscious brain. The vast number of crimes, homicides, genocides, suicides, bombings, killings, and human suffering results from our instincts. The vast majority of prisoners, jailors, offenders of domestic violence, and people involved in crimes and conflicts results from our emotional instincts. Even social issues, such as divorce, estranged relationships, egos, and the likes and dislikes, are subconscious choices. The subconscious wages false defenses, lies, and rationalizes at any cost to defend its motivations.

Our rational brain is at the forefront when we argue, talk, apply a reason to everything, and do what we think is right. It controls 100% of our rational thoughts, which constitute about 10% of our daily operations in life. The cerebral cortex is a soft, grey, gyrated top thin layer of the brain, which is newer and acts slower; the number and the density of its nerve cells are lesser. It is actually the tip of the iceberg whereas the subconscious is the mighty mass beneath the surface of the sea. The subconscious is the most powerful force in our lives, and it produces 90% of our behavior. It can be fast and furious, meaning that it carries veto power over our conscious mind, and it is the culprit for committing most violence, crimes, and incarcerations.

The subconscious mind unleashes our automatic behavior. It's older, quicker, powerful, and contains massive numbers of densely studded nerve cells. Our subconscious, more or less, decides our motivations.

Therefore, the subconscious mind overrides the rational mind. It is the commander-in-chief, which is the law of the land. It is evolutionary and built for self-protection and survival.

Outer conflicts are between individuals—like husband and wife, children, parents and children, and among co-workers or friends, etc. This conflict can also relate to social-economic classes, employees and employers, associations, unions, and organizations. Virtually every group in society has its self-interest, and each individual within the group wants to preserve his/her own against overall societal interest.

Self-interest is a major source of clashes. People want to grab everything available in the world. They cut trees, pollute, contribute to global warming, evaporate the thinning ozone, increase carbon footprints, and overall, cause environmental degradation. Our approach to nature is a clear example of an outer conflict.

Minimizing the Damages of Conflict

We should all be aware that conflicts are inevitable. The best thing one can do about conflicts is somehow minimize and deal with them. We can prevent them, act proactively, or reduce the damages. The first thing we can do is categorize the problem: Is it financial, emotional, or societal? Whatever the problem might be, you need to know exactly where the problem is. The second thing is knowing whether the problem is due to internal or external conflict.

As I've shared, I would see many young patients with lots of physical symptoms: feeling unwell, unhappy, and irritated. Testing and prescribing drugs wouldn't cure their illness. The only rational remedy was figuring out their inner conflict and offering a sensible cure. The most crucial thing in any dispute is de-escalation—like a ceasefire or negotiation. Most wars, in some form or another, reach the point where we stop fighting and start negotiating for things. The de-escalation should be done in two stages.

The first stage is a cool-off period. As we have discussed before, conflicts evoke and entangle emotions in the midbrain and nestle down in the cerebellum. We should call for a time out or ceasefire until the calm prevails in order to pursue rational choices. We can walk away from an argument and count down from 100 backward or put the issues on the back burner for a while, which is a simple, common-sense measure.

The second stage is untangling emotion from reason, which is a colossal challenge and equally fierce. How do you untangle? Typically, the feelings are so intense and so strong with control, and the subconscious is spewing itself through our tongue. Our negative self-talk affirms our emotional feelings into a bottomless, dark pit. It's very tough to break from the associations involved, which is where the problem resides. The solution is in there somewhere. Until you untangle everything, it's very tough to see—it was for me, which I'll share at the end of the chapter. Once you disentangle the issues from the emotions, you can settle the conflicts rationally. Every problem has a solution, whether you like the solution or not.

The third best thing we can do is engage in heart-to-heart communication with adversaries. Inevitably, this type of communication leads to building mutual trust, furthering discussions, and paving the way for the settlement of disputes. This conversation is possible only when you untangle negative emotions from the issue. Showing empathy to understand each other's viewpoints facilitates win-win communications and favorable results as well. Lightening up on self-imposed rules, principles, and attitudes is often helpful in resolving the tough problems.

As far as strategies for resolving the problem are concerned, I'm very big on what is called "win-win." principle. I will always look for this form of resolution. I think many people often misunderstand this principle. Win-win can be 50/50, 10/90, or even 90/10 win-loss between the parties in the dispute. Give and take in any proportion possible is a win-win. This principle not only paves the way for resolution but forges a relationship going forward for working together. Compromise is not a wrong term;

cutting the losses and resolving the issues earnestly earns peace of mind and happiness.

I implemented this principle and received massive advantages all my life in my medical practice and my relationships. Even today, I commit to win-win. Give and take is not a bad option because there are no winners if the fight continues. The result is mutual destruction. In the interest of avoiding that, a little bit of success for both sides is not bad at all. Using this approach likely will result in collaboration, cooperation, and arbitration.

I think the most important thing is to cut your losses and get out of any problem. Indeed, this approach is the secret of happiness in life. It's how I stay happy. I cut, cut, cut any loss quickly and remove myself from the perennial conflicts. Prolonging the issue only leads to further deterioration.

Overall, I keep the end in mind. It's important to know what you will gain and what you will lose: Will it matter? Can you look at other options? Can you look at the issue differently? There are many possibilities in any given situation. By keeping the end in mind, you can continue addressing different courses of action until a resolution is in sight.

Many conflicts can be prevented before they break out. If you are sensible enough and exhibit empathy, you can spot them. When you can see differences that could invite friction, you can then take care of them before they become big problems, which is about being proactive and aware.

I want you to know there is always a solution to every conflict. It's very important to believe in this dictum. When I worry, I always remind myself, *come on, there is a solution. It's just a matter of finding one.* That assurance is a great relief. Beyond finding a solution, conflict resolution lays foundations to building happiness—a very crucial point. With a conflict, you can never build happiness. Tranquility and peace, the antonyms for conflict, are essential in building your Vehicle of Joy.

As I've lived, I have discovered that conflicts can be resolved reasonably if you always have balance in mind. I'm a big believer in Buddha's middle path, Socrates' golden mean, and Confucius' moderation. I have always sought and followed the middle path for comfort and ease. If we want some excitement and adventure, we should expand the envelope and explore the horizons. The people flirting with the extremes swing to the fences, helping the average folks to identify and stick with the middle path.

Once reconciliation is accomplished, it takes time to heal and put the conflict behind you. No conflict should become a burden to grieve, resent, or avenge at any time. You must keep your mind clean from any previous dispute. A clear mind can cut through the issues creatively and effectively. Focus on developing trust that can further build future relationships. Keeping an empty mind to take fresh issues readily and making quick choices is the secret of my happiness.

Accepting Failure

The biggest problem in my marriage was accepting that it was a failed one. It was an internal conflict for me. The problem arose because I grew up in a small village where the custom, culture, and beliefs were that you marry only once in a lifetime. The concept of divorce was unheard of during my youth. When I moved to the west, I was faced with a divorce rate of 50%. Although I found myself in a new world, I never changed my mindset, belief, or faith in the old system. That's where my wheel of change got stuck.

It was an emotional tsunami for me. I shouted at myself often. I cried alone in my room. I felt lost, and I did not know what was going on or what would happen. I read an incredible number of books to understand what love is, how love evaporates, and why divorce happens. While my learning of new factors evolved, I continued believing that it was all because of my beliefs, customs, and culture. So, I decided to research those factors instead.

I read the vast works of many people. This time was transformative. I gained a deeper understanding of society. I believe that all beliefs, customs, and cultures are time and space-bound, but I took a long time to realize this fact. Everything is related to time and space, which is constantly changing—so too, everything is changing. But my mindset was framed between the 1960s and 1970s and based on rural Indian cultures and customs. It was stuck there even after I migrated to the west in the late 1970s.

It took months to study, during which I barely slept. I read every possible book. I had dizzy spells at work due to weight loss. Gradually, mulling over the issue for months, I concluded that three enemies were buried in my mind that caused my inner conflict.

My number one enemy was my old belief system, which was a head-on crash with the new western society where I had made my life. The idea of divorce leading to two people going their way to be happy never occurred to me for a long time.

My second enemy was my rational mind. I believed that reason and logic prevail in resolving problems. It came down to an idea I had during college. I used to think that life is like two chemicals interacting and that emotions would cool off with time. The results of that chemical reaction would then be the one that leads to life. It was a totally mechanical understanding of rationality. I paid the penalty for this notion.

I never realized the power of the subconscious mind. Throughout our marriage, unbeknownst to me, some emotional distancing occurred between us that I did not see. I lost her emotionally. In hindsight, I realized that I was ignoring the subconscious mind, which carries a veto power over the conscious mind. The subconscious has only a two-word vocabulary: either it likes or it doesn't like. It doesn't understand the rational language. If something is said that it doesn't like, that's all it needs to know—it doesn't matter what you said, why you said it, or how well you said it.

The subconscious mind controls our emotions, unconscious behavior, conditioned responses, anger, and outrage. Many incarcerations result from domestic violence, crime, and homicides due to subconscious rage. I believe relationship failures and divorce are largely rooted in the subconscious mind, which is yet to be fully humanized and civilized to control our behavior. It is the number one enemy of humanity today. Consciousizing the subconscious is a slow, tedious process that I will discuss in the chapter on affirmations.

My third enemy was a habit I developed in my school days. As a student leader, in the union meetings, I pointed out two sides of any coin at any time. I always believed there were two sides to everything. If something was going well, then I saw the part where things could go wrong. It's like playing devil's advocate. Alternatively, if something was going very badly, I also saw the part where things could have gone positively.

I thought this way was cautiously optimistic and a positive attitude, but that approach didn't seem to work well in intimate relationships. Back to the subconscious mind, if there is any indication, caution, or mention of negative feelings, on a psychological level, *it just sees the negative and doesn't like it.* Overall, these three enemies on my part, I believe, drove the emotional gap in my marriage.

Once I identified my inner enemies, I had a great awakening. I came to the reasonable conclusion that my conflicts were within my consciousness. The next day I woke up with a fresh mind, totally relieved with mental peace and tranquility. Of course, the sadness of my divorce still prevailed. I sat with my ex-wife to talk about everything. We had 22 years of marriage and a son; many other bonds beyond the wedding bound us. This conversation was the most dreaded one I ever had in my life.

Face to face, in a trembling voice and tears in my eyes, I told her, "We're not able to be happy together, so we'll go out in our ways." She thought about it and said, "Okay." She felt equally sad and fearful. As we spoke with each other, I told her that I could take care of myself, and I urged her to take care of herself as well. Even before marriage, I always had the best intentions for her. That feeling never left me. I told her, "We are still young. We can build happy lives again."

We ended our marriage peacefully as friends and only used one attorney. We were able to split a substantial estate without any dispute or further emotional damage. While the divorce was very sad, we were able to move beyond the conflict in peace.

Activity: Identifying Your Conflicts

Writing down conflicts crystallizes your thoughts and clarifies the mind. It gives you an excellent chance to understand and evaluate the problem rationally. If you keep thinking, it's very tough to get deeper and finalize the issues. So, journal it, identify the problem, set a goal to cure it, and write down how you will do that. Now, I want you to think of conflicts in your life.

In the first half, write your top three inner conflicts down on the respective top lines. They might be about your relationships, finances, job, peers, family, or friends. Below each conflict, write down the solution: strategies, risk/benefit assessments, or what-ifs while keeping the end in mind. In Part B, do the same for your external conflicts.

Inner Conflict #1: _____

Solution: _____

_____

_____

_____

_____

Inner Conflict #2: _____

Solution: _____

_____

_____

_____

_____

Inner Conflict #3: _____

Solution: _____

_____

_____

_____

_____

External Conflict #1: _____

Solution: _____

_____

_____

_____

External Conflict #2: _____

Solution: _____

_____

_____

_____

_____

External Conflict #3: _____

Solution: _____

_____

_____

_____

_____

After you complete this activity, observe yourself as you move forward. Review weekly progress and alternative strategies as needed. You might find new solutions for your conflicts as you work towards resolving them. In the next chapter, we identify the purpose of life and implement more meaning into our happiness.

CHAPTER 4
Stage 2: Identifying Purpose

The purpose of life has been debated for ages. For too long, the ordinary person looked up to the high priest, clergy, temples, churches, and synagogues for guidance about divine purpose. The people were advised to serve God and serve monarchies to meet that purpose. As social evolution took place, through the Great Awakening, the laws of Magna Carta, and the French Revolution, people have redefined purpose as the aspirations and happiness of the common person.

I was confused and frustrated by reading and listening to the religious elite, pundits, and pontificators. *What was purpose? Was it God-made or human-made?* And that was the general debate and discussion within. After reaching my conclusion of it being self-preservation and mutual help, I realized that this issue was not so clearly discussed in the community around me at the time. It took a couple of days for me to make sure that my definition of the purpose of life matched every philosophical, evolutionary, and social perspective of human thinking and doing.

When I found out the purpose of life could be distilled to a short phrase (self-preservation and mutual help), I experienced a transcending, exhilarating emotion. My conclusion was a thousand-bolt elephant light bulb in my mind. This definition clarified my priorities. At the top of my priorities is caring for myself. At the time, this priority was in descending order: spouse, dependents, family, employees, and society. Processing this clarity traded my conflict, anxiety, stress, and negativity for a peaceful mind, positivity, and happiness.

Loving Self in 2nd Place

Janet Smith was a slim-built, frail-looking woman in her late 60s. She moved to Florida from Detroit, Michigan, a few years before meeting me. In 1996, I saw her in our medical office for abdominal pain, gas, and diarrhea—mostly related to her chronic stress and anxiety. Janet lived a somewhat sheltered life under her domineering husband, who had recently succumbed to dementia. She also had a 40-year-old alcoholic, unemployed, and divorced son.

My physical examination and testing of her illness revealed that she suffered from Irritable Bowel Syndrome (IBS). Her family lived on a minimal retirement income along with Social Security. She worried about paying the bills as well as her husband's mental state and forgetfulness. Also, she was concerned as to how her husband was angered easily and threw temper tantrums. She tried to explain or reason with him. The effort it took was quite understandable because of dementia; but even before, he had a somewhat domineering personality.

Overall, Janet's biggest worries were her husband's mental state and her son's financial requests—he called her frequently. On a follow-up visit, I asked her, "Whose welfare is a priority in your family?"

She said, "My husband's health." I replied, "No."

She paused for a few seconds, and then she said, "My son."

Then, I said, "No." I saw that she was puzzled, but she had a dry grin on her face. I then asked, "How about yourself?"

This question prompted her to respond, "Oh no! I'm a Catholic. I was told to care for the family first and caring for myself is last." Janet couldn't believe what I suggested could be right for her. I told her if she stayed healthy and happy, she could help her loved ones much better and for a longer amount of time.

Janet is not alone in this type of situation. I have seen hundreds of patients who live in a constant state of fear, anxiety, and frustration with family conflicts—usually dominated by one spouse, often male. They suffer helplessly with stress and depression. In Janet's case, this conflict was leading to further suffering from IBS. I encouraged her to see the importance of her health and mental well-being, to see feeling good as her priority and the well-being of her loved ones as her second priority.

The Purpose of Life

I believe the purpose of life is delivered through goods and services we render to society. Anything and everything we do to make a living—whether you are an engineer, a doctor, a nurse, a senator, or a janitor—virtually any work anybody does meets their purpose in life. The same purpose is served by charitable or altruistic service—it's partly heritable and partly acquired. Human values, beliefs, faith systems, and lifestyles have evolved around the dictates of evolutionary needs. Your purpose is rendered in what and how you think and act in your daily life. As I've shared previously, a new, straightforward definition of the purpose of life is helping yourself and helping others.

Any work you do helps others as well as yourself. We make a living by earning a salary, making profits from businesses, or doing anything that we like. Any work you do as a profession serves the purpose of life. It is essential to realize that this purpose is equal; it doesn't matter how rich or poor, powerful or weak, intellectual or not—each of us does what we can, and we are equal in purpose. I think that's the humblest fact you can realize; otherwise, conflict, egoism, and stress begin setting into your perspective.

People strive to build a better world for themselves, their children, their grandchildren, and further descendants. In helping to build a better world for themselves, they are making a better world for others. How we go about that depends on our beliefs, values, and principles in life. However, it's evident in my mind, whatever you do, you're serving a purpose. Likewise, any idea, object, chair, book, house, ion, or atom has a goal of its own. Just knowing that we're serving a mission is very empowering as well as exhilarating.

Everything and anything you do touches millions and billions of people all across the lands, through your invisible hand. The perspective of an invisible hand was first introduced by a Scottish economist, Adam Smith, in the 18th Century. Regardless of what you do, be it a carpenter or engineer, professor or barber, president or janitor, you meet your purpose through your service. Just knowing you serve your purpose in life aligns your values, goals, and behaviors to it. Besides, it heightens your self-awareness, confidence, commitment, and performance at work. It also gives you peace of mind and empowerment.

Every service has an intrinsic or commercial equivalent value in the grand scheme of things. Therefore, the purpose of life overrides all the social distinctions of class, hierarchy, authority, status, pay, and skill. I've defined two types of purposes, but in the final analysis, they both serve humanity from different directions. The first one is self-preservation.

We all know that self-preservation is the first law of life. Every living organism, including humans, wants to preserve and survive. Airlines across the globe recommend putting oxygen masks on yourself before your child in the event of an emergency. Self-help is not selfishness; it is self-preservation — an evolutionary mandate and a birthright.

Self-help or preservation is not greed, and greed is the polar opposite of self-preservation. Each of us must exercise our conscience, moral values, and systems to differentiate between self-preservation and greed. We work hard to become wealthy, healthy, and happy; perhaps sending our children to schools and colleges to develop their skills is a priority. In the case of raising children, we prepare them, get them married, and then they procreate and so on. The purpose of this cycle of life is to preserve and propagate humanity.

The second aspect of the purpose of life is helping others—which can be seen as mutual help or interdependency. That simply is people helping people. It's done for the three most important reasons:

1. Sharing
2. Mutuality
3. Ancestral Debt

Sharing is a human need and creed. We share our genes, origins, planet, universe, breath, air, water, etc. People are grouped into families, tribes, communities, nations, classes, and associations to share and flourish together. We partner with one another to join forces to protect our self-interest—and, in the end, to help each other on (as) groups (mutual help). Our ancestors hunted and gathered together in groups. They shared tools, food, and shelter because together, we win; divided, we lose.

Mutuality is mandatory for human survival and propagation. Man and woman procreate and protect their offspring until they can lead an independent life. The five-feet, hundred-pound human hunted and gathered and lived in groups to leverage the strength of mutuality to fend off the wilderness, natural disasters, calamities, and many other risks in life. No matter your profession, you will touch over 7 billion hearts and minds. Your service flows invisibly in quantum leaps across the continents.

I'll mention the September 11th terrorist attack on the World Trade Center as an illustration. It catalyzed world trade, travel, and the economy for decades. One single terrorist attack flattened the trajectory of the world's progress for decades. Man is not an island. Either we flourish or perish together; exist or become extinct together. That's the power of interdependency.

Lastly, we received an ancestral debt from previous generations; it's our moral obligation to pay it back to future generations. Our ancestors built a beautiful modern world for our enjoyment. We are wealthier, healthier, happier, and lead secure, comfortable lives because of their sacrifice. They worked hard, explored lands, revealed wonder, mystery, and fantastic life. They developed science and technology. Thousands of revolutionaries and reformers gave their blood, sweat, and tears for our sake as well as produced life, liberty, and the pursuit of happiness. We're morally obliged to embellish in our generational gift and hand it to future generations.

Whether you self-preserve or help others, it remains community service. Therefore, "The purpose of life is to be happy," as Dalai Lama said. Overall, focusing on being happy and serving the purpose of life is intrinsic to humanity.

Purpose of Work: Who do you work for?

Miss Sofi is my assistant in the endoscopy room. One day, instead of the usual welcome greeting, I saw her turn to a corner of the room and mutter, "I am furious and upset. I wish I could quit my job right now."

I looked at her for a few seconds and asked, "What are you upset about?"

Miss Sofi complained to the director of endoscopy that her assistant wasn't cleaning the scopes per protocol, risking cross-infection to patients. Instead of taking action on the employee, the director of endoscopy told Sofi, "If you want a clean scope, you better do it yourself." So, Sofi was upset and unable to focus on patient care.

I asked Miss Sofi, "Who do you work for?"

She fell deathly silent for a few seconds and resumed her work.

Conflicts, miscommunications, arguments, and disagreements with a boss, manager, or colleague are frequent at work. We should distinguish the purpose of work (function) from that of the administrative conflicts (structural) to respond rationally and responsibly. A nurse in conflict with her boss should not allow her loving care of patients to suffer. A president of the United States of America in conflict with Congress over building a border wall should not shut down the government to punish the federal employees.

So, your service should be identified, which is purpose. Acting with a distinction between the meaning and the means helps us with handling conflicts, frustrations, and anxieties at work and makes them more manageable. And, just to be clear: helping others isn't limited to money or donations. You can help others through spending time with them, counseling, expressing gratitude, offering an apology, or extending unconditional love—and giving gifts, smiles, hugs, and sharing happiness. As you do such things, don't forget to help yourself as well.

Loving Self in 1st Place

Janet's goal was to get over her immediate problems and then establish long-term goals and affirmations. As I continued to see her in my medical office, I reaffirmed her top priority was to care for herself. She read my newspaper articles about the purpose of life, exercise, stress management, achieving inner peace, happiness, etc. She framed her goals and affirmations to recapture her self-esteem and well-being. She set her goals to resume daily walks, go out with friends, learn to say "No" to her son's requests for money, not worry about or get frustrated with her husband's indifference and remember that caring for herself is not selfishness. It took several months before the idea of self-care sunk into Janet's mind because she was indoctrinated into a different life by her place of worship.

On one of her follow-up visits, I asked Janet if she was accepting my advice about self-care. She sported a smile with a glitter in her eyes. She gained self-esteem and felt much more comfortable making choices without feeling guilty. What was the purpose? Caring for herself became the priority while giving the best of herself to her loved ones. Janet continued to help her husband and even her son, but she did so without fear, frustration, and stress—so much so that her physical illness eased up.

Janet took daily walks, ate on time, and went out with friends. These little things throughout her everyday life made her sane, and she felt much better. When her husband's health further deteriorated, Janet put him in a nursing home and visited him regularly. She learned to say "No" to her son when she could not afford to help him financially. While she struggled with this before, Janet knew she was doing right by herself with the help of the new value system. She overcame stress and depression and gained well-being and happiness. She continued to help her son and husband just as before, if not better. Janet earned her freedom and independence to live happily, fulfilling her purpose in life.

Activity: Identifying Purpose for Yourself

I recommend that you sit down at a tranquil moment and reflect on your deeds to figure out your purpose. This is a writing exercise, not just a thinking one. Again, writing crystallizes your thoughts, reaffirms the commitment, enhances focus, and lays down the roadmap. Write down what you do to help yourself, and write down what you do to help others. This list isn't limited to your job. It could also be homemaking, child-raising, community service, and any form of service, touted as the purpose of life.

A. Self-help: Write down what you do to stay healthy and happy, at work or home (i.e. your engagements with family and friends to feel good and enjoy life):

_____

_____

_____

_____

_____

B. Connect how what you do for a living helps others, visibly or invisibly (directly or indirectly):

_____

_____

_____

_____

_____

C. Write down your charitable community activities (i.e. donations, volunteering, cheering up or expressing empathy, love, and gratitude to others):

_____

_____

_____

_____

_____

D. Journal the encouragement, help, compliments, and support you get or give to others at work or home daily:

_____

_____

_____

_____

_____

Now that I've further explained the purpose of life, it's time to launch into Stage 3. In Chapter 5, we work on setting our goals as well as understanding their value and purpose. Once our goals are set, the path to building our happiness will be much more precise. Let's put the body on our Vehicle of Joy!

CHAPTER 5

Stage 3: Setting Goals

The above diagram depicts that goals fuel our successes in life,
as burning propane gas enables a hot air balloon to fly away.

Is goal setting necessary? It wasn't relevant for hunters, gatherers, or farmers in the early stages of humanity, as their lifestyle options were minimal. The fundamental desire to survive and thrive was intuitive to biological evolution, and it was always on their mind. However, the modern world has changed. We experienced massive material, social, and psychological progress, all leading to a complicated, sophisticated lifestyle.

Indeed, advances in material comforts, specializations, and consumerism as well as higher expectations have contributed to a life full of options. Similarly, globalization, open markets, rapid communications, outsourcing, and the internet revolution have mushroomed into many opportunities and possibilities to entertain and enjoy life, including decisions such as:

- Which school or college to attend
- What subject to study
- What job to do
- Where to live
- Whom to marry
- How to enjoy life

Goal setting was born to answer these questions, to create a purpose and plan for one's life in a complex world. It has become the standard for individuals, groups, associations, enterprises, and even political parties and educational institutions to make mission statements—the public setting of goals. In truth, acting at random without goals or priorities is akin to being a kite in the sky with a broken string.

A goal is a roadmap to an action that fulfills one's wants and needs. It is thinking about the ideal future and planning for it, making choices about what you want in life and accomplishing them. Goals should be self-directed, fulfilling, challenging, and achievable. Imposing arbitrary rules, hours of work, and pushing for profits are not purposed goals in my mind—that is an external imposition. Goal setting should focus on creating value for the customer.

Psychologists Edwin A. Locke and Garry P. Latham proposed internal goal setting, and their work has reported its success. Their criteria were for the goal to be specific and un-intricate but challenging enough to be able to achieve it as well. If you abide by Locke and Latham's definition of intentions, it works better performance-wise than simply instructing the workforce to do their best. The goals should be challenging, and people should be motivated as well as skillful enough to do those jobs.

I want you to understand and accept that goal setting has become a necessary standard of life to succeed. There's strong empirical evidence that people who set goals earn more and live happier than others who don't. Goals are a roadmap only, not a fixed post or a path. We need to be flexible and creative along the course of action. Our goals should align with our purpose, beliefs, value systems, resources, and skills.

I recommend that you share your goals with family, friends, and peers. Doing so reinforces your resolve. It also affirms your commitment to taking your goals seriously. Never fear failing in goals; in my mind, failures are a stepping-stone for more significant successes. Goal setting helps build happiness and leads to living free and fearless.

Training of the Body

(in exchange for that of the mind)

Mark Weber was a muscular, tall bodybuilder in his mid-thirties. He migrated from West Germany and lived in his Dad's vacation home in town. I hired him as my personal trainer in the summer of 1995. As we got to know each other, he shared that his goals at the time were to find a second job, make more money, and buy an apartment or a house of his own. Mark was also interested in dating girls and meeting the right one to marry. He had other goals, like working out five days a week, going on a weight-reducing diet, and losing 20 pounds in 12 months.

As he made an effort to change his life, Mark made sure to keep expanding his mind. He read well and was interested in self-improvement literature. At the end of our training sessions in my home, he discussed that literature with me—whatever he read on the previous day. He attended my seminars, workshops and read my newspaper articles. While he trained my body, I taught Mark how to live happily. We both had a lot of fun in this exchange. He's a disciplined, principled person with a clear purpose and priorities.

The Moral Approach to Setting Goals

Goal setting becomes a worthwhile venture for the people willing and eager to go after achievable but challenging tasks in their lives. The setting of goals for its own sake, without serious commitment, becomes another wish or hope-filled expedition developed during birthdays and New Year. Sit comfortably in a tranquil place to reflect on your successes and failures thus far and plan to set up your goals for the short and long term. Make a comprehensive list of your health— which includes mind and body, exercise, emotions, diet, education, work, relationships, and finances.

Your list should include essential goals about the major domains of your life. It will take a few weeks to resolve inner conflicts, complexities, and uncertainties before you can finally form your goals and priorities. Consider having optimal opportunities at your disposal. Think of abundance and dream big while you set your goals. Financial and retirement planning issues should be dealt with as long-term goals; they might take five to ten years and sometimes, a lifetime.

Writing down goals deepens your clarity and commitment for the purpose that you're pursuing. Eliminate conflict in your goals. Often, once you think of some goals, you'll find a conflict between them or within each goal. For example, if you want to make more money, take an extra job; sacrifice the time you would typically go out and do leisurely things—spend your time in a different way. Basically, money and time cut into each other in such situations. Likewise, you must be very careful when you choose the goals; each of them should not conflict or eat away from another's resources.

The general recommendation is the criteria for SMART goals:

- Specific
- Measurable
- Achievable
- Realistic
- Timely

Thinking lofty or thinking of a large number of goals is irrelevant to this activity. You can set any goal. You can set all kinds of goals, even modest ones, as long as they are a target to achieve. So, your goals should be specific as to the time, how you want to obtain it, and when you want to make it. They should be measurable; your goals should have proper metrics and monitoring—weekly, monthly, or daily variations.

The attainability of goals means that you don't just hook up a ladder to the sky and hope things will happen. Again, the goal should be challenging enough but reachable; still, your goals should be meaningful to you and fulfilling your purpose in life. Similarly, they should involve time in their conception—in a sense, there must be a time in which it's possible for success. Your goals should not be out of place or context.

The benefits of goal setting have been well established through empirical evidence as well as personal experience, including my own. For this chapter, I focus on the following benefits:

1. Awareness
2. Organization
3. Mindset
4. Time Management

The first benefit of conscious awareness is the most important, super, powerful engine within oneself. Most people act on subconscious instincts motivated by egotism, not from conscious awareness. But choosing our goals rationally, matched with our purpose and passion—knowing why we do, what we do, and how we do—raises our self-awareness as to precisely what we're doing moment to moment or in whatever actions taken in life. This awareness boosts our core strength, self-confidence, peace of mind, and pride. It's empowering and enjoyable.

In terms of organization, again, goals lay out the roadmap for our life. Goal setting channels our past, desires, and wants into an actionable path. It delineates the roadmap to organize our vision and mission in life, which accomplishes decision-making and prioritization, making it easier to balance money and resources with your goals. The setting of goals cascades focus and commitment as well as gives you the means and the meanings of rations.

Thirdly, goal setting launches a mindset, which is a very fundamental idea. People should have a mindset in which they are ready to move into action. Most people are confused, fearful, or frustrated; by causing people to take any action, goal setting overcomes that problem. Mindset is the most energy-efficient mental tool one can have. It negates inertia, procrastination, and confusion. Our behavior is automated and repeats itself like a broken record. It vanquishes flexibility or change of mind until you tune it differently. So, the mindset can help or hurt us; it's a double-edged sword.

An example comes to mind with my physical trainer Mark. He habitually kept his home clean and tidy. He had set his mind to clean the house after work. When Mark arrived home, his wife (spoilers, as some say) asked him to take her out for dinner. He declined her wish as he had set his mind on cleaning the house that evening.

The next morning at my training session, Mark asked me, "Doc, why won't my wife appreciate a clean house?"

From my experience, I quietly questioned the wisdom of his priorities. "Is keeping your wife happy a priority, or is a clean home a priority?"

Indeed, Mark could have done both if he managed to keep a flexible mindset and considered his wife's request. It would have been smart to keep the mind flexible to entertain final hour changes in life. Rigid mindsets squander possibilities whereas flexible mindsets engage all of the new opportunities.

Lastly, goal setting is a time management tool. We can only manage, not control, our time. Squeezing everything into every minute of the day stifles creativity, innovation, and spontaneity. Whereas, goal setting should be productive, stress-free, and effective to spare time and resources. It is doing the right thing, at the right time, in the right place, while keeping the end in mind.

Goal setting has many other secondary benefits. It negates fears and frustrations because it is action-oriented and positive. Thus, it attains control over building our future. Achieving goals turbocharges our self-confidence, optimism, and happiness.

The Framework

A general framework of goals includes the following:

1. Self-Preservation
2. Mutual Help
3. The Mind
4. The Body

Our goals should consist of self-preservation issues like basic needs, finances, health, and security. Likewise, they should include doing common good like helping others, charitable actions, and building relationships. Goals should also include issues concerning the mind, like learning every day in every way to promote Neuroplasticity. Other items for our goals concern issues of the body, like exercising, walking, practicing yoga, and meditation. Building relationships with family, friends, peers, and co-workers also should be included in goal setting to enjoy life.

I had no idea about setting goals through my education and career. The concept of goal setting struck my mind once I became a very busy medical practitioner. When I had too many things to do in a given time, the need for planning and prioritizing came naturally. For reference, I share a journal entry from January 1, 2001:

> **Physical:** exercise an hour for five days a week. Diet: avoid milk and milk products as I am lactose intolerant. Watch my weight *(which has been stable, fortunately, but I still decided to watch it anyway)*. Mental: self-discipline. Wake up at 5:00 am, write daily from 5:15 to 6:15 am. Work out from 6:15 to 7:15 am. And then go to work.
>
> Read two books a month. Improve writing skills *(this is my handicap; I was never a writer, and I did not have the vocabulary or grammatical skills to write. So, I decided to improve on them).*

Write articles to newspapers and give talks. LT (*meaning long term goal*): Attain financial freedom by the year 2005. LT: Create an income stream to live comfortably.

Associate with successful people and about leisure and pleasure. Play golf (LT): bring down my handicap to 80 (*which I have yet to reach*). Swim three times a week. Travel one national and one international trip a year. The goals for medical practice were to work without mental stress and physical distress. Recruit associate doctors into the practice and delegate the work to them. Focus on personal relationships with referring physicians.

My personal experience continues to show me that goals work. No question about it: setting goals is how you anchor your life plans, both long term and short term. For me, it wasn't just about writing them down, but memorizing them is a handy tool in implementing goals because they were on my mind at all times.

Many issues, confusions, and conflicts come into our minds. Screening our problems through our goals one by one could help us find solutions much sooner. Goals tend to have a snowball effect. They gather bits and pieces of small mass in the beginning, but they accelerate at a greater mass accumulation as time goes by.

I accomplished most of my short-term goals within a year because they were easy to measure and monitor. My long-term goals took nearly a decade to break through most of them. Beyond goals set in that journal entry, I've had many new areas of success. There were many things I succeeded in that I never even thought about—for example, starting two charitable organizations, Awareness USA and Chaitanya Saradi Trust in India. Being creative and trailblazing your path while working at your goals will lead you through the path of least resistance to new opportunities. Our self-growth and wisdom may blossom into different things that we never previously considered. Our goals should not hinder easier paths or better opportunities.

Prioritizing and Screening Goals

Prioritizing and screening goals is the ultimate action in goal setting. The world is fast, but life is short. We must sort out tons of available options to pick a few goals that are achievable and can be matched to our values and resources. The effective execution of our goals is where time being money becomes very complex and confusing. Pareto's principle states that 20% of our activities will account for 80% of our results. Therefore, prioritization is the answer to this paradox.

Prioritize with purpose in mind. People and organizations go bankrupt due to a lack of purpose and priority. It's essential to know the real importance of each competing goal. Which ones are important? Which ones are not? What is urgent? What is mundane? Which ones can go on the back burner? What steps are preventative? And which ones are accumulative?

Prioritizing is a dynamic play of shifting, juggling, mixing, and matching goals with resources. As I mentioned before, be mindful of the conflict between money and time. Likewise, be aware that the power of relationship is a greater influence on individual happiness and success than currency can buy.

After prioritizing, it's time to screen your goals. Analyze them with the following questions: Are your goals comprehensive? This question means there is something to be gained in terms of health, wealth, relationships, work, etc. Do your goals feed balance and happiness in your life? Some people go after the single goal that meets their success, risking the failure of their relationship or marriage. Sure, they might make tons of money, but at the loss of love—what good is that?

Do your beliefs, values, and ethics match your goals? That question is important too. You may work all your life and miss that aspect, which would be very sad. Do the goals serve your purpose in life? Are you grading and monitoring the progress and successes? If you don't, it's very tough to revisit, re-plan, and reinvigorate those goals. It is also important to share your goals with your family, friends, peer, etc. to clarify to yourself, without any inner inhibitions, what you want to achieve in your life.

Post your goals at work and home, having them staring at your face to remind of them regularly. Make index cards with your affirmations on them and carry them in your pocket or wallet. Put your goals on your screen saver. Share your goals with family, friends, and peers. This is all done to enforce your determination and affirmations in taking action. The most important thing to ensuring that your goals stay on your mind is memorizing them. Ensure that you review your goals daily.

Setting Goals for Happiness

Mark was effective in attaining his goals. He secured a second job at a car dealership to sell new cars. He saved up money to rent an apartment initially and then he bought a three-bedroom home in a good neighborhood. Mark fell in love with a girl after a few unsuccessful trials with others. They have a child who is about 12 years old now. Mark continued to train me for 15 years. He worked out regularly and managed to lose weight as he set up to do.

Mark is a success story. He fulfilled his goals in 4 to 5 years' time. He lived by his affirmations and value systems, which led to happiness. He is a great support to his community, and he coaches kids at soccer games. Mark donates money to feed the hungry and teams up to help Habitat For Humanity in building homes for the homeless.

Activity: Setting Your Goals

I want you to write down your goals. Follow the SMART Goals, as recommended in this chapter. Your goals should be comprehensive—meaning financial, physical, and mental. I then want you to prioritize them according to their level of importance. Then, I want you to screen your goals against your purpose and beliefs periodically. Be specific about exactly what your goal is as well as when and how it is going to be accomplished. In your goals, be sure to include ones that cover your needs in the following categories: financial, health, professional, travel, diet, and exercise.

Non-Prioritized Goals (for screening)

_____

_____

_____

_____

_____

_____

_____

_____

_____

Now, prioritize them:

1. _____

2. _____

3. _____

4. _____

5. _____

6. _____

7. _____

8. _____

9. _____

10. _____

Now that I've explained how to set your goals, it's time to move forward into Stage 4. In Chapter 6, we explore the concept of finding opportunities at the very roots of problems we encounter every day. Once we can accomplish this, our Vehicle of Joy will have a steering wheel, and we will have more control as we drive towards the future.

CHAPTER 6
Stage 4: Changing Problems to Opportunities

Life presents opportunities and challenges to everybody in society equally, but people view them differently. One's problem is an opportunity for another. When someone sells stock in the market for a loss, another is buying it for profit; the same stock trades for loss or gain. Someone is fired, and another is hired for the same job. The heartache of a broken relationship culminates in lasting, lovely friendships.

In the circus of life, a problem mindset can be traded to a growth mindset if we have the will and the skill. Going to school and studying, finding a job, learning skills, or disciplining oneself through hard work fulfills our personal need to excel in life, but for some, these are problems. Considering problems as opportunities is the difference between success and failure. I present my experiences in developing an opportunity mindset in this chapter.

In the Oxford Dictionary, a problem means "a matter or a situation, regarded as unwelcome or harmful, needing to be dealt with and overcome." The idea of a problem evokes body defenses, alerts the mind, narrows focus, and negates creativity and innovation. It diverts resources and efforts to defend or flee and stifles opportunities to think about what can be done going forward. The notion of a problem instills anxiety and actual fear in the mind whereas the word opportunity is defined as "a set of circumstances that makes it possible to do something." An opportunity is something to think or do to go forward.

The idea of an opportunity expands the mind, broadens vision, and provides the creativity to seek out the best possible outcome. The concept of opportunity evokes a growth mindset. This mindset is essentially free-associative thinking, to create and innovate new opportunities. Cognitive psychology taught us that we could re-engineer our thoughts, words, images, and imagination from a problem orientation to an opportunity mindset.

I want you to think rich and dream big. Our society is affluent enough to offer material comforts and healthy lifestyles. The world of knowledge is at our fingertips. Never dream (regret) about the last opportunities; go after the new ones. This entrepreneurial world is changing at a dizzying speed. If you wish to optimize your chances, then get on skates and ride along time and space to garner them.

Thinking big is an essential concept because unless you feel that there are abundant opportunities, you'll be restricted to a scarcity mindset, and that's not the world that we live in today. Education has lifted the tide of human progress. All the wealth and good health we enjoy today—comforts, luxuries, safety, security, etc., —are the products of education.

Education has mothered our wealth, health, equality, liberties, and fairness; it accelerates everybody's upward social mobility in the world. Opportunities abound if you can master the skill and knowledge of the opportunities available in society. Even when you are settled in life, continuing learning or education should be chosen because it invigorates the trajectory of your future lifestyles and happiness.

Building strong relationships with friends and peers in society is the most influential source of opportunities—and that has been the case in my life. Getting breaks in life is a measure of who you know and how you are connected to them. Most of my opportunities came from my social connectivity. So, associate yourself with successful people. Our relationships are a measurement of our money; otherwise, what we own, how healthy we are, how happy we are, and how long we live are in part linked to our relationships. Opportunities gravitate to the people who are positive, trustworthy, approachable, and helpful.

A Lone Breadwinner

Samantha Johnson was a 30-year-old, slim built registered nurse who was referred to my office on January 15, 1998, for bloody diarrhea. She was known to have ulcerated colitis, which had relapsed and failed to respond to the medicines prescribed to her. I admitted her to the hospital to administer drugs intravenously. Samantha improved and was discharged home after two weeks. She was working for a busy private medical practice in the county before she became ill. They had fired her and hired another nurse in her place, so she was jobless.

Samantha was the breadwinner in a family of four young children. Her husband did odd jobs but mostly stayed home to help with the kids, schooling, and housekeeping. She visited me following the hospital discharge and was literally in tears due to the loss of her job and income. Samantha was also worried about paying off the hospital bills and my bills as well as buying medicines.

I gave Samantha some samples of medicines to get by on for weeks and waived my fees. I called the local hospital administrator whom I happened to know well and requested that he consider hiring her for a vacant position they had in the hospital at the time.

Problems VS Opportunities

The first thing we must do when faced with a problem is get over the first impressions. When we confront unexpected events, emergencies, catastrophes, or setbacks, our initial reaction is shock, wonder, surprise, feeling overwhelmed, loss, and sadness. It takes some time to let the dust settle and think over what the real problem is and how to solve it. We must assess and define the type of stakes involved with the issue: What is the benefit/loss ratio? What is the risk/reward ratio? What is the first thing you need to do for the rewards you can gain?

Take a deep breath and let the emotions settle in time. Keep an open mind and find out what happened and what remedies you can offer to the problem. At every twist or set back, you can pick up the useful pieces, cut the losses, and get on with your new adventures. For example, Alexander Fleming's discovery of penicillin was a fluke. His experiments failed, but he noticed that a patch of the mold killed the bacteria on a Petri dish he had put aside a few days ago; that's the story of the discovery of the first antibiotic penicillin in the world—which saved millions and millions of people in the hospitals as well as during WWII.

Albert Einstein said, "We cannot solve our problems with the same level of thinking that created them." I follow this principle regularly. Look at issues from either higher or lower levels of creation of the problem. Look from different viewpoints. Try looking at them humorously sometimes, or collaboratively, or sarcastically, or even revel in the issues. Pass it to your mentor, coach, peer, or kids or spouse. You'll be surprised at the perspective you receive. It lightens the severe situation and allows you to take it easy; it enables the problems to simmer on the back burner. This approach provides a better chance of spotting opportunities.

It's critical to create an opportunity mindset, which can be used in how you interpret and respond to situations in daily life. People fall into either a problem mindset or an opportunity mindset. The problem mindset is a problem itself. It cascades negative emotional burdens, stress, and an escape from reality. This perspective sees the problem everywhere, encouraging you to give up easily; it encourages a reluctance to change and adapt.

Opportunity seekers, on the other hand, keep an open and flexible mind to learn and adapt to new realities. They expect and deal with routine problems, emergencies, and setbacks as an unavoidable nuisance. They view issues in a positive, easy manner, which reduces the burden and stress in their thinking. The opportunities can be spotted when we are in a happy and creative mode, but never when we are depressed or stressed.

An opportunity mindset seeks the possibilities and approaches problems with a win-win solution as an option. They can compromise. They are comfortable with conciliation. Sometimes, they even forgive and forget. Looking for solutions alone often creates a lucky break when faced with any problem.

Beyond problem and opportunity mindsets, always keep the purpose in mind while looking at the conflict. Search through all arguments and disputes, whether in relationships or business, and try to figure out your purpose. This approach allows you to release problems related to egos, spite, fame, power, or dignity. Purpose delineates them out of your equation. Assess the downside as well as upside along with the risk/reward ratios—and remain open to cutting your losses to spare those resources for new ventures.

Something that I believe is effective in this process is looking at problems without the notions of right/wrong or good/bad. Look at the issue as a matter of differences, not with any fixed rules. Remember, all the current realities are partial truths; they morph with passing time and space. This thought is a philosophical concept that will render much softening of mental attitudes regarding any severe problems.

A Snatched Seat

As I've shared, I was a farmhand for a year after fifth grade. I would have been a lifetime farmer, save for my older brother putting me back in middle school when he became a teacher. In the summer of 1963, I was one lucky high school student to have graduated. I dodged failing. Even then, I required grace marks from the headmaster to graduate. I wouldn't have been admitted to college, but a relative lent me the tuition fee at the last minute. I was then elected to join the Veterinary School of Medicine after college. Unfortunately, a Government Minister snatched my seat for his nephew in the final hour.

My fortunes were ruined overnight. I felt rejected and depressed. Then, I took the same college course a second time and was admitted to Medical School. I never dreamed of becoming a Doctor. I have no words to describe the overnight elation of my fortunes, pride, and prestige. It was a twist of my fate. The disappointment of the previous year ceded an outlandish opportunity the following year.

I wouldn't have finished medical college but for the tuition-free government education, scholarships, and financial aid from a generous donor. I read the quote from John Adams that "Every problem is an opportunity," which profoundly influenced me during my medical practice. I read this quote when I was busy at work and expanding my practice.

In every problem I encountered in my medical practice, business, or relationships, I looked for the opportunities as per this quote. Even the very thought of this quote lightens my heart and shakes up the problem mindset. It feels funny if not hilarious to think that way in some situations; however, I entertain it at every problem.

Opportunities aren't always apparent at first sight. Therefore, I revisit the issues several times in search of hidden jewels—whether direct or indirect, short term or long term, tangible or intangible benefits, etc. Sometimes, I cut the loss and run away from it. An opportunity mindset helps to avoid problems and seek better opportunities and a better future.

Again, we live in an affluent world that offers abundant opportunities; therefore, there is no reason to be boxed into your conflicts. Move away from the hot spots to safe havens and start doing what you love to do. As shared in Chapter 3, I have a certain attitude from my college days:

I spot the positive and negative aspects of every problem—both sides of the coin. I then take my position on the positive side.

I was happy seeing many patients and working late hours in the day because I was making money. I was equally pleased when I saw a few patients a day because I was enjoying leisure. Eating a sumptuous meal was my pleasure, but I felt similarly contended eating less tasty meals lightly, which helped me to control my diet and weight. I tend to see both sides and accept things as they are. I always think about the next move in good, bad, or worst situations. Thinking this way is a warrior mentality; if you lose the right hand in the trench war, you fire with the left hand, and when you can't walk, you crawl. I then consider future actions and how to take the opportunity further in some way or another, doing something different.

Turning Problems into Opportunities

There are six necessary steps to this process:

1. Untangle emotion from the problem
2. Check the problem in different ways
3. Find a job that you love
4. Find your purpose at work and be creative
5. Embrace the fact that every question has a solution
6. Create a to-do list

1. Untangle your emotions

This task is a primary necessity before you can spot opportunities. Problems originate from the emotional or rational side of the mind. They soon merge and mingle with each other. Our negative emotions taint, entangle, and malign issues big time.

People fabricate wrong reasons and develop illogical arguments to defend their subconscious motivations. When you are angry or upset, a defensive mode kicks in and goes into higher gear, which puts you in a place where you are unable to take any opportunities at that time. The rational mind requires a tranquil, balanced, and creative mode to entertain opportunities. That state is possible only after we unbundle the negative emotions and false realities from the root cause of the real problems. It's impossible to look at opportunities when you are upset.

2. Check the Problem

Look at problems from different perspectives to explore potential opportunities. Albert Einstein's famous quote, "No problem can be solved from the same level of consciousness that created it," is true in my experience. Analyze the problem: explore motivation, reason, logic, and emotion. Categorize the problem: such as a health, work, business, financial, or relationship issues.

Quantify and qualify, and prioritize the issues: split them into urgent, critical, or mundane, short term or long term, trivial or life- changing, and overt or covert. Then, check the consequences of each issue, keeping the end in mind. Checking problems gives us a better chance of sizing the issues realistically and spotting opportunities and solutions going forward.

3. Find a job you love

Whether you are employed or own a business, you should love your work like a consummate dancer, carpenter, or artist. It's impossible to build an opportunity mindset without enjoying the work you do. Negative energy is what kills one's growth, development, and other potential creative behavior. It all comes to a halt. Passion alone in doing what you do isn't enough. Therefore, I encourage you to look at the contribution. I believe the love of labor and contribution often ride together. When they drag you in different ways, go along with your contribution, and the love of its labor will emerge in due time.

4. Find your purpose at work and commit

In the grand scheme of things, any work provides the meaning of life. All working people serve society knowingly or unknowingly, willingly or unwillingly. Relating your purpose at work dispels doubts, fears, and conflicts in that environment. Knowing the meaning of your actions boosts your psychological health, well-being, and performance.

5. Every problem has a solution

The modern world offers abundant opportunities to fulfill your dreams, aspirations, and lifestyles and to find solutions. The issue isn't the scarcity of possibilities; it is overcoming one's self-limitations. If you lost your job, you can find a better paying one, and you might even be able to work from home. If you ended up in a broken relationship, amend your attitude to build a better, long-lasting, loving relationship. If you lost money in a venture or lost power or control, you can rebuild all that much stronger than before.

Even a heart attack heralds one's discipline to stop smoking and drinking excessively—and go on a diet and practice weight control. If you hit a bad golf shot, you know what not to do for the rest of your rounds. The setbacks are challenges for greater excitement, success, celebration, gratification, and glory in life.

6. To-do list

It's a good idea to prepare a to-do list and act accordingly. For example, you can make a list of things to do the night before or in the morning before daybreak. You can then have this list on hand, stick it to your work desk, or put it in a screen saver or on your smartphone. Amid busy schedules, emergencies, distractions, and interruptions of any day, it is easier to remember to do your routine chores.

Our memory and attention have a short span. Referring to our to-do list reminds us to help accomplish whatever task(s) we set for the day. Recent scientific studies have shown that striking off the items as you do them pumps up the happy juice in your body. More importantly, it creates new energy to look at new opportunities.

The Breadwinner Gains

Samantha was interviewed by the hospital administration and hired for the job as a supervisor. It fetched her higher pay than her previous job. Besides that, she also gained health insurance coverage and medication coverage. So, Samantha has a career, her health, and her life back. For several years, she visited my office for her chronic ulcerative colitis, and she attended several of my life management seminars. She set her goals and affirmations to maintain health and finances.

Samantha's story illustrates that an opportunity for a better paying job and perks surfaced only after the status quo was disturbed. I continued to see her until I retired. She remained a passionate nurse taking care of the sick and wounded.

Opportunities surface when problems are present. When a person is struggling with issues, many supporting hands can chip in based on the person's relationships. Indeed, potential opportunities lurk around us continually. We simply need to know how to spot and grab them.

Activity: Identify Your Potential Opportunities

I want you to jot down a list of problems you encounter in each domain of your life—health, work, relationships, etc. Then, look for the right solution and write down potential opportunities you can explore to resolve your problems and find further opportunities.

Problem 1: _____

Opportunity: _____

Problem 2: _____

Opportunity: _____

Problem 3: _____

Opportunity: _____

Problem 4: _____

Opportunity: _____

Problem 5: _____

Opportunity: _____

Now that I've shared how we can turn our problems into opportunities, it's time for Stage 5. In Chapter 7, we choose affirmations that will fortify the previous four stages. Before this Vehicle of Joy hits the road, we need an engine in place!

CHAPTER 7
Stage 5: Choosing Affirmations

"THE POSSIBILITIES OF THOUGHT TRAINING ARE
INFINITE, ITS CONSEQUENCE ETERNAL, AND YET FEW
TAKE THE PAINS TO DIRECT THEIR THINKING INTO
CHANNELS THAT WILL DO THEM GOOD, BUT INSTEAD
LEAVE ALL TO CHANCE."

—Brice Marden

Affirmations aren't a new concept. People have been practicing affirmations for centuries, but they didn't necessarily call them affirmations. For example, Christians and Jews pray three times a day, traditionally—not necessarily all the time. Muslims pray five times a day—pretty strictly. Buddhists meditate daily for hours. Hindus do yoga and read Gita. People of all cultures celebrate their customs, rituals, mysteries, and myths to reinforce and reaffirm. Lovers idolize and fantasize while terrorists long to be welcomed to paradise after their death—they do it by reaffirming their beliefs and faith.

How do affirmations work? Affirmations build our habits, attitudes, and behaviors by developing new neuroplastic networks in the brain. We are habit creatures—90% of life and living is carried out by our subconscious mind. Practicing self-affirmations over time helps our conscious thoughts gravitate to and embed into our subconscious, where they become emotions and feelings. The goal of this enterprise is converting conscious thoughts into attitudes, habits, and behavior. This automation saves energy and time, and it improves performance.

Mental conditioning or habit formation requires reinforcement through self-affirming talk, prayers, songs, chants, or meditation. The human mind can be trained to become an angel or a devil. Athletes focus on training mentally using affirmations and visualization techniques, which are also part of a type of affirmation. People use this self-improvement technique in any field, personal and professional. Affirmations empower your ideas, beliefs, and actions, positively and negatively; whether you want to become a saint or a serial killer, they assist you.

Adolf Hitler used mental conditioning to brainwash his fellow citizens to carry out genocide. Tamil Tigers, leader of the Prabhakaran, used this technique to create suicide bombers for the first time in human history. Al-Qaeda, ISIS, and similar religious sects use the same mental conditioning to brainwash their followers into committing inhumane crimes.

Affirmations are concise, self-taught statements that "firm up" what you intend to believe, focus on, value, or do. They are built around your beliefs, values, goals, and priorities to streamline your perspectives and actions for life. Using them will boost your core strengths while helping you avoid distractions and deviations. Therefore, in my mind, affirmations can help in building an enjoyable life.

There is nothing to fear about affirmations. They do not take extra time. They actually save you time. Affirmations turn your thoughts and actions into automated habits, attitudes, and skills—which can help you conserve time and resources. Before you start any given activity, you must take many, many steps. By making new habits, you avoid procrastination, confusion, distractions, and deviations in making choices and taking action, which is the ultimate purpose of forming your affirmations.

Affirmations are easy to set up and practice. You can do them anytime. There's no need for training, gurus, or master trainers. They are inspiring and empowering; they emotionally support you as positive psychological tools. They are the engine in our Vehicles of Joy. You can scale your affirmations to build the desired horsepower, torque, and efficiency of the motor of your liking.

The Debt of Gifts

I hired Beth Fowler in her mid-forties to manage our endoscopy unit in the winter of 1998. She was a tall, blond, hardworking, loyal employee who had a constant urge to impress her boss. She had three adult children and two grandchildren. Beth was the mother goose, caring for and protecting her family, financially as well as emotionally. Her children had issues with money and drugs.

Beth suffered from bipolar depression and anxiety. She generously bought Christmas gifts for her family, incurring big credit card debts; this debt later brought further stress and suffering to her life. Beth was in perennial credit card debt, paying thousands of dollars of interest for years. Therefore, she set a goal to be debt-free in five years and asked for my help. I offered to pay off her debt with an interest-free loan from the medical practice, which would be payable in installments at her convenient time.

Beth believed that she should please the bosses to keep her job safe. In her efforts to do so, she became defensive, emotional, and put down her subordinates. Often, I told Beth the best way to impress the boss was to be good at work and help the practice grow. She attended my seminars, read my newspaper articles, and had direct access to counseling at work. So, Beth formed affirmations:

1. "Do what is good for the medical practice, not for trying to impress the boss."

2. "The best way to impress the boss is to improve billing/ collections/public relationships and build good teamwork."

3. "Separate emotions from the issues."

The Necessity of Affirmations

We live in a rapidly changing and complex world. The capitalist economic system—open markets, competition, consumerism, and incentives— where time is money, drives people crazy. Growing wealth, affordability, and lifestyles—luxurious cars, mansions, jewelry, attire, fashion, and comforts—combined with ease of borrowing compel people to spend much more money than they can afford. This spending results in many people incurring debt, which is often further exacerbated by social obligations, holidays, birthdays, anniversaries, and marketing gimmicks.

Modern life is complicated, stressful, and challenging. Market globalization, commerce, and outsourcing have created massive worldwide opportunities and complexities. Running from pillar to post— or simply wishing, believing, and praying—gets us nowhere. Therefore, we need a set of affirmations to lead us through modern confusion and challenges.

First, affirmations simplify and clarify your thoughts in regards to choosing your goals and values. Also, they fortify, strengthen, or boost your commitment, focus, and action in cherishing your goals. Affirmations are based on your core strengths to excel and succeed in life, so your focus becomes more targeted.

Memorizing affirmations is a must. When affirmations are always on your mind, you can use them at any time of the day. Most importantly, when you get in trouble, face a problem, or find yourself worried about something, you can immediately recall the most relevant affirmation for the situation. This ability has been very helpful for me. Unquestionably, affirmations have ignited building a happy life over a while.

Neuroplasticity and Habit Formation

What is neuroplasticity? Brain tissue is very malleable, like plastic, and it will change according to the thoughts, ideas, and skills you want to promote. The nerve cells and their networking in our brains are adaptive to the changing thoughts and practices in our daily life. New thoughts and practices wire our brains to acquire new habits, attitudes, and behaviors. Likewise, the neurons and their pathways undergo disuse atrophy as the old habits die, which is called neuroplasticity. Affirmations fire neurons to wire together and reinforce the nerve cell junctions and neuronal networks, which means every time you repeat your affirmations, it recruits more nerve cell junctions and strengthens the neural pathways for faster learning and firmer memories.

Attitude, habit, and behavior formation

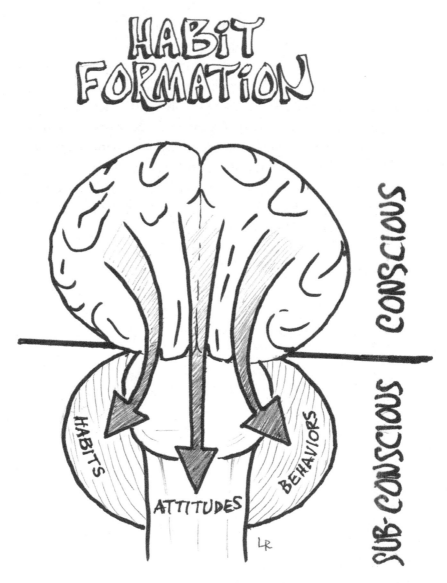

The above diagram shows how affirmations work their way down to the midbrain to blend with emotions, and then migrate further down to the Cerebellum to manifest new habits and behaviors.

The nerve cells produce a chemical —a neuropeptide that can activate the cell surface receptors over long distances in the body. In a Google scholar article, "Molecules of Emotion: The Science Behind Mind-Body Medicine," (New York, 1997) Candace B. Pert, Ph.D., stated, "As our feelings change, this mixture of peptides travels throughout your body and your brain. And they're changing the chemistry of every cell in your body." They create new emotional memories and experiences and impregnate them in the midbrain. By practicing the newly set affirmations, they migrate down to the second level of the brain, which is called the midbrain, where stronger emotional memories and feelings of the declarations are etched in the amygdala and hippocampus. This process builds stronger declarative memories capable of creating an experience and feeling every time that message repeats in the mind.

Now, the embodied feelings from the midbrain finally nestle down at the bottom part of the brain, which is called a third brain or cerebellum. Without our conscious effort, the cerebellum retrieves and processes long term memories of the embodied feelings to manifest our habits and behaviors when a particular thought comes to mind. Otherwise, when you say an affirmation repeatedly, it will go through this process, eventually forming permanent, long-lasting, and subconscious habits, attitudes, and behaviors.

In his book *Breaking the Habit of Being Yourself*, Dr. Joe Dispenza writes, "The cerebellum stores certain types of simple actions and skills, along with hardwired attitudes, emotional reactions... and skills that we have mastered and memorized." The role of the cerebellum is elevated to be a microprocessor capable of taking massive data from the prefrontal cortex and sensory systems via midbrain to feed back to the cerebral cortex.

This process is the beauty of habit and attitude formation. We can do things without thinking, which is how the subconscious mind controls 90 percent of our daily activities, attitudes, habits, and emotions. The downside of this efficient conditioning is like a broken record, the same behavior repeats regardless of changing times. People get stuck with old habits and attitudes. When they behave in ancient ways in a new beginning, their behavior and attitudes become outdated.

The remedy is reversing these exact processes called consciousization: stripping away emotions and feelings from attitudes and habits to reexamine and amend them to fit ongoing changes in society. Undoing or changing habits takes greater due diligence and harder work than the habit formation. More discussion will follow on this issue.

Pillar to Post

My personal experience with affirmations started in the winter of 1990. Why did I bump into self-affirmations? As shared in Chapter 2, I was three years into my new life in Crystal River, Florida, and I was working on my goals to build a successful medical practice. I worked very hard from morning to midnight, seven days a week. I commuted 70 miles on a daily basis between two hospitals and two medical clinics. Thoughts of growing my medical practice came and went from my mind without me reflecting on doing anything. I ran from a pillar to a post in a rat race, without vision and mission. I never had a chance to sit back, relax, or grow my thoughts or actions.

In the midst of this storm, I took a skiing vacation to Breckenridge, Colorado. Watching the slopes, I had an epiphany. I wondered what the heck I was doing with my life. *Do I enjoy what I do? Should I be working this hard? Are there any better and easy ways to practice medicine? Can I ever find joy in practicing medicine just as the people skiing the ski slopes?* As my mental fog cleared slowly, clarity stepped in.

I thought of an article I recently read about the benefits of self-affirmations. I decided to write a list of my own at that moment. This activity dusted off my mental clutter and confusion. It was the most accelerating and empowering moment in my life. My long-lasting list of affirmations was born by the end of that vacation.

I have taken affirmations from my diary that I used to practice in September 5, 1997:

1. Have a great day, every day.

2. Learn every day in every way.

3. Feel free and fearless.

4. Review my goals every day.

5. Turn every problem into an opportunity.

6. See both sides of the coin and act on the positive side.

7. Use 100% of my brainpower.

8. Expand the envelope and engage in new horizons.

9. Enrich my sense of humor.

10. Consciousize my subconscious.

Note: The word consciousize is not in the dictionary yet, but I thought it was a good verb. It means you are increasing awareness of your subconscious deeds. It is the verb form of the noun consciousization. I expound on this concept shortly.

These affirmations opened the door for hope, optimism, and enthusiasm. They projected charm and handsomeness within me. I actually whistled while working. Some patients, as well as some of my nursing staff, were surprised that a doctor who worked so hard managed to whistle and be happy. Happiness is an infectious charm; it ignited happy faces and great relationships.

I assumed many leadership positions, and my practice grew big-time, from a solo practice to a seven-member group. We provided service to most of the county. I stood tall and brave. I looked attractive. I smiled. I was poised and had good posture. My affirmed personality had a great influence on how effectively I was able to build relationships and succeed in my life.

A Great Day, Every Day

My first affirmation was "have a great day, every day," and it is the most powerful affirmation in my experience; I still use it today. My day starts by greeting everyone with a firm handshake and gentle eye contact while stating, "I feel great." As I say it, I stand tall, thrusting the chest out with my chin up and the crown of my head chasing the sky. This ritual empowers me all day long. My mind reverberates with courage and confidence. I feel and act like a hero in a movie. The beauty of it is that each routine encounter becomes a positive, compelling engagement, an outstanding ploy of public relationships and a formula for success.

If I happen to slip into a bad mood or remorse, saying this affirmation boosts my morale, emotional feeling, and well-being. I recommend saying affirmations repeatedly in a private place, loud and clear, until your mind is resurrected back to your usual self. I would not recommend doing this in public; I'm sure you would feel the difference.

The recent discovery of "mimic neurons" explains how your emotions, feelings, and moods affect others around you. A child's cry saddens and glooms parents' mood. A spouse's lousy mood worries his/her partner. Subordinates approach their boss when he or she is in a good mood to effectively ask favors. Positive and negative emotions are equally infectious. Exhibiting positive feelings and enthusiasm in public is a tangible source of contributing to others in society. You don't need to hide your emotions. If you are happy, say it. If you are in a good mood, say it. Say it to anybody—privately, of course.

Below are some phrases I've heard others use to express the same feeling. Find your phrases or pick up any one of the following. Let them imbibe into every cell in your body.

- I don't know what I would do if I felt any better.

- Feels like I'm in heaven.

- I'm in seventh heaven.

- I'm on top of the world.
- I feel happier than a pig in mud.
- I feel outstanding.
- I feel peachy.
- I feel handsome.
- I feel beautiful.
- I'm living my dream.

Consciousizing the Subconscious

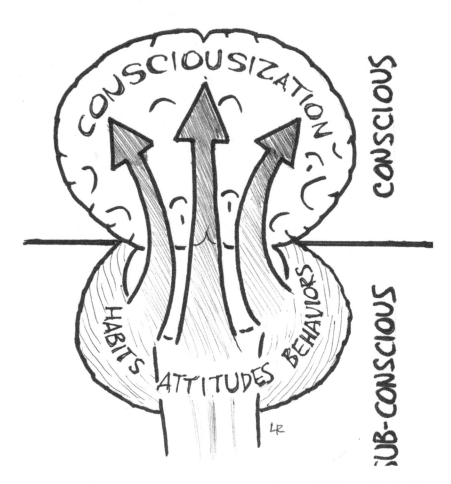

The above diagram of consciousization shows that our habits and behaviors occur when we walk back precisely on the path of habit formation (i.e. we will have to strip emotions of our actions and reexamine them rationally).

As discussed earlier in this chapter, affirmations transform our thoughts into our habits, emotions, and behaviors whereas consciousizing reverts your attitudes, habits, and behaviors to awareness. This act comes down to knowing what, why, and how you do things in daily life.

Again, we are creatures of habit. We acquire our attitudes, practices, and behaviors from our parents, family, friends, peers, teachers, society, and the old world. In the rapidly changing world, past generational attitudes and behaviors become outdated. Newly evolving socioeconomic trends and conditions require a newer set of attitudes, habits, and behaviors. In olden days, when the world wasn't changing much, old was gold, but during rapid change, the old gold turns to dust fast. Moreover, what you learned from others isn't your own.

When you begin to know who you are—your likes, dislikes, preferences, and fancies—you begin to wake up to living your life. This awakening is called self-realization. Then, you need to amend your old attitudes and habits. This self-realization takes you to the summit of total freedom and happiness in life.

You can live life wallowed in the dictates of the old world, or you can choose to liberate yourself from the past and start fresh with what is your own. Self-realization requires a fair amount of dismantling of old attitudes, habits, and behaviors. Once you get through this dismantling, you can begin building a set of updated, self-realized beliefs, and a conscience to manifest your personality. You should examine your attitude and behavior thoroughly, closely, and critically and amend them to fit your conscience and will—that is a realized happy life. People are often stuck in their past habits, attitudes, and suffered fears, frustrations, and stress—this is an unrealized stressful, unhappy life. The only way to liberate oneself and live free and fearless is to live a life of one's own.

Be critical of your habits, attitudes, and behaviors; question what and why you do what you do. Getting lost in conditioned response isn't the goal of self-realization. You can consciousize your fears, frustrations, worries, stress, emotions, and feelings. This act can enable you to untangle emotion from reason, fact from fiction, and imagination from reality. You can journal about any of these issues for several weeks, and beneficial patterns of thinking and behavior will evolve that you never thought about before.

Question your fears, worries, and frustrations as to why, where, when, who (etc). In thinking that way, you will be able to examine your behavior pattern fully. Question the intent and purpose, and discard or modify as you feel necessary. Your assumptions, knowledge, and wisdom also need to be questioned internally so that your conscious mind approves of those behaviors and actions going forward.

By accomplishing synergy between working parts of the brain, you eliminate things that are not yours and build a bridge between your conscious and subconscious, which eliminates inner conflicts and allows for more quiet times. Breaking old habits—eating bad food, drinking excessively, using drugs, stealing, committing crimes—is tougher than working to build new, healthier habits. Still, this must be done.

Something to think about is that this process is the same in reverse. Affirmations turn our thoughts into habits; consciousization, on the other hand, can strip down the emotions of habits for a pure rational reexamination of our thoughts.

Setting Up Your Affirmations

Sit down and relax in a most peaceful place, in a conducive environment where you can think about what you want in life. Reflect on your job, health, wealth, family, relationships, and purpose. Write down all the affirmations that come to your mind, based on your goals, values, and beliefs. There are plenty of declarations available. Indeed, search online, but be discreet—pick only the ones that match your aspirations. Don't go too crazy, writing too many of them. I think 10 is an okay maximum; less is better.

Write them down in concise, simple, direct language. And, always write them in first person, present tense so that they will have a direct impact on your life. Enter them in your journal or diary or record them on a CD or iPhone. Post them on a desk at home or the office so that you can readily see them. Don't be bashful about your affirmations. If people share or take them, that's fine—that's another contribution you're making to the rest of the world.

Beyond making them visible, I recommend memorizing them. I never, ever got the full benefit out of them until I did that for myself. Before I memorized, I would forget doing the affirmations for days, sometimes weeks. After memorizing them, I was able to remember to practice them regularly. Now, I have formed a habit of practicing my affirmations daily.

From Debt to Happiness

Beth understood the value of goal setting. She paid her loan back in over five years without any interest and attained financial freedom when she used my loan. Beth now makes enough to live debt-free, even though borrowing, being so lucrative, makes it easy to fall back into old habits.

Beth took the time to understand the purpose of her work as providing quality patient care, not pleasing the boss. She struggled to get over that notion over the years, but eventually, she was convinced that her job security rested on her performance at work, not the other way around. Beth retired after 20 years from the endoscopy center and currently works in hospice care.

Activity: Choosing Your Affirmations

Write down your affirmations and memorize them. They should be comprehensive, including mind, body, finance, travel, reading, and learning. And, they should be based on your strengths. I recommend that you also write a diary as to what you are learning each day. As you use your affirmations, practice body posture and poise; try watching yourself in a mirror. Also, as you think of your affirmations, stretch in the morning so that you can feel good and revel in them. Try saying them very loud in a closed room—shout them to the sky. All of these actions translate into real emotional feelings, and they integrate the body and mind to feel good for the rest of the day.

Affirmation 1: _____

Affirmation 2: _____

Affirmation 3: _____

Affirmation 4: _____

Affirmation 5: _____

Affirmation 6: _____

Affirmation 7: _____

Affirmation 8: _____

Affirmation 9: _____

Affirmation 10: _____

Now that we are embracing the inevitability of conflict and change, we know our purpose, our goals are set, we are changing our problems into opportunities, and we have chosen our affirmations, it's time to drive our Vehicle of Joy to the summit of happiness. As we enjoy the ride, we will meet many people along the way, and it's important to pay it forward whenever we can. In Chapter 8, I explain the importance of committing to charity, which I believe to be a moral obligation.

CHAPTER 8
Committing to Charity

People are social beings. We've worked, collaborated, and cooperated for the common good since the dawn of human evolution. Hunter-gatherers gathered food and protected themselves from large predators through united action. We help our neighbors, friends, siblings, peers as well as the poor, homeless, hungry, and even strangers in need.

We give or take, borrow or loan, and return favors in daily life. We live together as families, tribes, communities, and nations to preserve and prevail in life. We share happiness, sadness, success or failure, and celebrate birthdays, anniversaries, festivals, holidays, and even grieve together for the wounded and dead. Nations preserve their borders, security, wealth, health, and happiness for their citizens.

The concept of the common good, mutual help, and interdependency is an evolutionary dictate. We need to join together to help each other for the common good. When the community can't exist, the individual becomes extinct. Contributing to charity adds a final frontier of protection for the most desperate and needy among us. The underlying primary preface to humanity is to safeguard the community's prosperity, safety, security, and happiness so that an individual can thrive and prosper in it. Ignoring the common good erodes the individual's survival, safety, and security as well as that of our descendants.

A charity is a non-profit entity that uses money, time, or resources—such as teaching or providing training—for the benefit of the public without expecting any reciprocation. Charities help the hungry, homeless, disabled, and control or cure diseases in society. Americans gave $420 billion in charity in 2017 alone. Charity does not always mean "a charity;" for the purpose of this chapter, I simply mean giving, which can be emotional support, hugs, kisses, love, and comfort for those in pain and suffering.

Committing to charity is innate to human nature. It is a cardinal rule for human survival and progress. The good life you enjoy today is built on the hard work and sacrifices of past generations and working people. Let us accept contributions and express gratitude to ancestors, explorers, adventurers, scientists, reformers, and revolutionaries for building this wonderful world for us. They worked hard, risked their lives, and endured pain and suffering to build the modern world.

Giving money is not a criterion for charity. I don't want you to have that impression because you can give your time, emotional support, empathy, gratitude, or alleviate pain and suffering within your community.

An Inspirational Leader

Mr. Vasireddy Venkat Rao, an 84-year-old retired teacher, has been busy helping people all his life in India. He is my mentor and was my counselor during school and college. He helped countless students, teachers, friends, and institutions. He worked with various charitable endeavors, including the Lion's Club, as well as transported corneal transplants voluntarily to hospitals for years while holding a regular job. At 80 years old, my mentor accepted the position of CEO to The Chaitanya Saradhi Trust that I started in India.

Venkat Rao lives by an ethic set by an Indian saint, Kabir Das, "What you have to do tomorrow do it today, what you have to do today, do it now." He is a very quick, positive, inspirational leader to teachers and students in the program. I received some of his positive personality traits, such as self-drive, positivity, resourcefulness, and friendliness. Only recently, I realized this was the case, but he is a great inspiration for the man I am today.

We Are All Cousins

Modern humans, Homo sapiens, evolved in Africa 100,000 years ago. For many years, several thousand Homo sapiens clustered around the equator in East Africa to survive the brutal cold of the Ice Age. As the weather improved, they explored the lands and migrated to North Africa. About 50,000 years ago, a cluster of North Africans ventured across the Red Sea to Yemen and along the coastal way to India, Southeast Asia, Australia, and the Pacific Islands. By land, another group of Africans headed towards the Middle East, Southeast Central Asia, and spread out to Europe and central Asia. About 20,000 years ago, some East Asian arctic hunters crossed the land to the American continent, when the oceans dropped 300 feet below the current sea level during the Ice Age.

It took approximately 10,000 years for them to populate the entire North and South America. The paleontological, anthropological, and genealogical evidence concludes that all people around the world are cousins— anywhere from the 1st to the 5,000th degree. If we can realize and live by this truth when dealing with a conflict with any person, we would be more considerate and more likely to apply a win-win principle to make everybody happy. Helping a cousin in need with money, emotional support, and encouragement is an instinct and a moral act.

Humanity Shares Everything

As I've mentioned, we all share the same resources and life on earth. We even share life and death. We share genes, the earth, sun, universe, air, environment, emotions, and happiness. We share knowledge, wisdom, skills, and tools to help each other to protect, thrive, and live a good life. A man and a woman live together to raise offspring until the child is, or the children are, independent. Families, tribes, communities, and nations share national resources, knowledge, and wisdom for the common good.

We share and work together to prosper; if we don't, then we will perish. We will go extinct if we fail to protect the environment, water, air, and nature. Sharing is a charitable deed. We share wealth, health, natural calamities, and disasters—floods, fires, tsunamis, earthquakes, etc. Therefore, sharing is an act of togetherness, which is why we should help each other.

The Modern World is Our Ancestral Gift

I touched on this topic at the beginning of Chapter 1. Our species, the Homo sapiens, are much smarter and more curious than their extinct cousins. Homo sapiens have explored, adopted, and exploited nature to survive and progress. They have developed tools and skills to hunt together and lived in groups for reproductive and survival advantage. They discovered that cooking helped their food supplies by three times, and they used fire to keep themselves warm. They domesticated plants and animals and built ancient civilizations that laid the foundation for the modern world that we enjoy today.

Then came the Scientific Revolution, Age of Reason, The Great Awakening, The World Encyclopedia, and a series of socio-economic reforms and revolutions culminating in human freedoms, equality, civil rights, life, liberty, and the pursuit of happiness. The rapid developments that fueled the industrial revolution were followed by a series of scientific and technological advances ending in the internet and communication age we are in today.

This advancing generational collective consciousness of human knowledge is being recycled as it snowballs through generations. Our job is not only to use it to our benefit, but to also improve its content and recycle it back to society for future generations. Whether a millionaire, billionaire, a middle-class person, or a minimum wage-earner, each of us is thriving on the backs of our ancestors and their contributions. Therefore, we owe a sense of gratitude, and giving back to society is our moral obligation.

The Mother of All Human Progress

I believe education is the mother of all human progress. I also believe education alleviates pain and suffering from all socioeconomic ills. My approach to charity is not just giving money or resources; it involves using my mind to mentor, guide, or counsel people.

In 2010, I cut back my time in my medical practice and invested in reading and traveling around the world. For five years, I tried to figure out the kind of program I would undertake for the benefit of the public. In 2015, I retired fully from my medical practice and started Awareness USA and Chaitanya Saradhi Trust in India.

Everywhere in the world, people are hungry and eager to come and take advantage of the opportunities in America. However, millions of people within America are at the lower social-economic level and somehow do not use those facilities or opportunities to build their lives. This reality bothers me, and I am passionate about motivating others to rise up to the American dream, work hard, and build their lives.

Over the years, I've mentored high school students. One student, in particular, has remained my mentee for three years, and he is working hard towards becoming a doctor. As I believe education to be the mother of all human progress, I have helped scores of college graduates to pay tuition—especially those who come from India.

I grew up poor, resenting socioeconomic inequalities, and longing to help the poor and downtrodden. I am a passionate supporter of women's rights, children, the disabled, the working class, and minorities. I have made donations to various causes. As I sometimes have concerns about high overheads and the bureaucrats, I have reservations donating money to standard popular charities. I help people in my proximity when they are in crisis and have urgent needs.

As I've shared before, I confidentially loaned interest-free and easy payback money to several of my employees at different times for replacing a leaky roof, A/C units, broken radios, car tires, or to pay off consolidated credit card loans, etc. Most were single mothers without any savings to pay for their emergencies, and I felt passionate about helping them. They expressed great gratitude and loyalty because of that, and as a result, I built a strong team at my practice.

Our medical office mission was to care for all patients regardless of their financial or insurance status. We never engaged with collection agencies and wrote off many thousands of dollars of patient debt. That goodwill spread by word of mouth to help our practice grow very fast. I counseled our patients for stress reduction and motivated high school students when they came to see me for medical reasons. I also advised many families, friends, and colleagues engulfed in conflict and crisis. For several years (as shared in Chapter 2), I ran public stress reduction seminars, workshops, and wrote a series of newspaper articles and a booklet called "A Blissful Life: A Way to Reach."

Family Estate VS Community Estate

Families who work hard and save money become wealthy and live comfortably. The world is growing more affluent in advanced, developing countries and creating sizable family estates. We pass wealth to our children and grandchildren through wills and trusts, which is fair and what I do as well. A news item, "Riches To Rags In Three Generations," was posted by *The Trust Company's Family*

Office Services, on March 6, 2019. It reads, "Today, sobering statistics continued to show that the children and grandchildren of their fortune-building parents will lose 65% of the wealth in the next generation, and 90% by the following generation."

All citizens share the same national wealth, fresh air and water, open lands and sea, pristine nature, infrastructure, national parks, and libraries, etc. So, every American is much richer because the nation is prosperous. The world's intellectuals and talent gravitate to the US to share a piece of the pie. Building a stable, healthy, wealthy, and harmonious society makes all citizens more productive and provides greater opportunities for a better life. The historical data shows the community estate grows continually and helps everyone equally.

If you are concerned about your great-great grandchildren living safely and securely, you would be better off building a strong, wealthy society rather than just depending on handing down a big estate to your descendants. There is more value in building a community estate than building your family estate and passing it on. Moreover, neglecting the poor and downtrodden creates conflict and crisis. Therefore, helping fellow humans blends the self and the mutual interest for the common good. So again, I argue charity is a moral obligation.

The Benefits of Charity

Giving to charities produces physical, psychological, and emotional well-being. Interestingly, the feeling of gratitude is common to the giver as well as the receiver. Giving promotes a strong immune system, lessens body pains and aches, reduces blood pressure, improves sleep, and provides further intentions to exercise more often. There have been scientific studies proving that charitable people are not only happy and healthy, but they also live longer. If people start giving in their 20s and 30s, they can live eight years longer, and those who start contributing after their 70s apparently live two more years longer. One such study is titled "Happy older people live longer" by Choy-Lye Chei et al., published on August 27, 2018, in *Age and Aging*, the scientific journal of the British Geriatrics Society.

Helping people is enjoyable, gratifying, and fulfilling. No wonder people risk going to prison, starving, being tortured, or even becoming suicide bombers to help their communities. If it weren't for their faith and passion for building a better world for their progeny, many of the wisest explorers, scientists, freedom fighters, reformers, revolutionaries, and philosophers would not have spilled their blood, sweat, and tears. Likewise, figures such as Moses, Jesus Christ, Mohammed, Buddha, Mother Teresa, Martin Luther King, Jr., Nelson Mandela, Karl Marx, and Mahatma Gandhi staked their lives to shape a better world.

Human Diversity is a Thing of Beauty

(it shouldn't be a cause for conflict)

Human migration and isolation to different parts of the world from Africa have given birth to independent people and diverse cultural, linguistic, regional, and religious identities among us all. For example, ancient civilizations and agriculture started about 10,000 years ago in different regions of the world have developed differently. Likewise, different faiths, and lifestyles have evolved in different parts of the world about 5,000 years ago. Whereas, the three monotheistic religions (Judaism, Christianity, and Islam) had evolved from common ancestral roots.

Likewise, the caste system of India is about 2,000 years old; it began with two castes that evolved into many castes and sub- castes. We lost numerous cultures, subcultures, rich heritages, and things of beauty from genocides, killings, wars, and repression. We have lost Native Americans, Mayans, Incas, and hundreds of aboriginal groups and cultures.

These different nationalities, cultures, customs, faiths, languages, and political systems were a thing of evolutionary beauty. The diversities have evolved to fit with their nature and survival (i.e. natural selection). Distinctions between people based on preferences came to light much later. Diversity added the color, flavor, and beauty of nature to humanity. Understandably, people fought for their identities when they didn't know they were cousins. Knowing what we know now, I hope people will embrace diversity instead of exploiting it for personal or political gains.

Legal Entitlements

(a moral corruption)

Governmental entitlements and handouts somehow killed some peoples' incentive to work hard. Unfortunately, some people got used to the benefits and made a living out of it without working. Handouts to the needy are necessary to overcome an immediate crisis, but long-term benefits unwittingly have encouraged people to depend on them, ending in generational poverty. Indeed, extreme entitlements and equal distribution of wealth killed incentives to work hard and crumbled the Soviet empire. This issue needs leadership that can face the problem squarely and provide practical solutions.

Helping people in need will not result in moral corruption. Indeed, it results in gratitude and love. Political issues or social challenges should not hinder people from wanting to help people. We can help those affected by earthquakes, floods, fires, and starvation—where the immediate needs are necessary. There is any number of other causes, like education, research, disease control, prevention, and environmental protection, etc, for people to donate to help.

Building a Better World

While Vasireddy Venkat Rao worked as a full-time teacher, he raised two daughters and two sons to become responsible, productive citizens. In doing so, he met his evolutionary responsibility. He found success in his personal life, including financial independence and happiness. Currently, he works as a full-time public servant, as I shared at the beginning of the chapter.

Venkat Rao and I travel and work together in India. He is an inspiration to me. No other emotional or psychological satisfaction is greater than helping people in need or building a better world. When I travel in India and give motivational speeches, I feel very thrilled doing that type of work. We are trying to mentor younger generations in building a better world. Venkat thinks that his life is fulfilled through serving the community, and he enjoys his life immensely— the same can be said for me.

Activity: Focus on Your Charity

I want you to write down how you give or receive, whether it is help, charity, or service to others. Focus on the feeling of gratitude, empathy, and understanding; doing so will become a good character builder and motivator for changing. Also, I ask you to write thank- you note because scientific psychological studies show that writing these notes regularly or expressing gratitude is good for health, well-being, and longevity of life.

Below, write down the charitable acts you do, in any form: money, time, volunteering, emotional support, and communal or familial support.

Charity 1: _____

Charity 2: _____

Charity 3: _____

Charity 4: _____

Charity 5: _____

Charity 6: _____

Charity 7: _____

Charity 8: _____

Charity 9: _____

Charity 10: _____

In the last hundred years, the world has seen so many changes that are equal to the last hundred thousand years of development. I epitomize that change. Imagine a kid as poor as I was in a small, little village in India. Today, I am on par with—I'll unashamedly admit—the top percentile of the population in the world. So, what caused my transformation? What made me come this far? It's all because of millions and millions of hands at every level pushing me up. I hope that you will see the hands supporting you in your life.

Now that I've explained how charity is a moral obligation—and at that, one worth committing to—we are ready for the last chapter. At the center of Stage 5 (Choosing Affirmations), I shared a list of my affirmations, one of which was "I feel free and fearless." In Chapter 9, I share what it means not just to feel, but also to live in such a way. If we work together, driving our Vehicles of Joy as one, then anything is possible.

CHAPTER 9
Living Free and Fearless

"I LEARNED THAT COURAGE WAS NOT THE ABSENCE OF FEAR, BUT THE TRIUMPH OVER IT. THE BRAVE MAN IS NOT HE WHO DOES NOT FEEL AFRAID, BUT HE WHO CONQUERS THAT FEAR."

—Nelson Mandela

From Stage 5, my "feel free and fearless" affirmation is not about fear; it's about being fearless and free. Feeling free rings, the bells of freedom, individualism, independence, and self-realization. People who enjoy what they do feel the passion and the courage to enjoy life.

Modern society offers all the elements required to live free and fearless. People in the west and developing countries have attained financial freedoms. The world's wealth, health, material comforts, safety, and security have improved, increasing the plausibility of living free and fearless. World poverty is dropping fast (about 10%), starvation is vanishing in a hurry, and disease and disasters are better prevented or controlled. The world's nations are free and independent. People enjoy freedom, liberties, individual rights, and constitutional protections. People are free to travel, live where they want, love whom they like, and do what they love while making a living.

Freedom is not just the right to paint, speak, or write, nor is it exclusive to gathering together, praying, or using public places for walking and transportation. Freedom also includes social and economic rights. As I've explained, the freedoms we enjoy today are a precious generational gift. We should be grateful to heroes, explorers, reformers, revolutionaries, and visionaries who sacrificed their lives to build a prosperous, safe, secure, peaceful world for us today.

Death of Socrates

The seeds of modern freedoms can be traced to Socrates, the Greek philosopher, who questioned youth in the streets of Athens about freedom, democracy, and the role of the government, etc. For Socrates, the freedom of speech was stronger than the fear of death. He drank poison to take his life, as sentenced by law, instead of giving up his freedom to speak. The spirit of freedom took a major leap forward about 2,000 years later. Many thinkers, reformers, and revolutionaries ignited the age of enlightenment.

Feeling Free

John Locke, citing the Law of Nature, argued the government's job was to serve the people and protect life, liberty, and property. He pleaded for the rule of law and denounced tyranny. Around the same time, German philosopher Jean-Jacques Rousseau promoted a political philosophy that fermented the start of the enlightenment era and the French revolution. Likewise, Voltaire, Montesquieu, and many others pushed for freedom of speech and rights for ordinary people, the rule of law, checks and balances for state power, and separation of church and state.

Look at the Declaration of Independence of America:

> "We hold these truths to be self-evident, that all men are created equal, that they are endowed by their Creator with certain unalienable Rights, that among these are Life, Liberty, and the pursuit of Happiness."

Americans are such a fiercely independent people; feeling free and fearless is their nation's capital. It feels great to feel free and brave. Having the freedom to think, act fair, and do as you please is enjoyable and should be a fundamental right of global citizens in the modern world. This emotional and psychological state unleashes the creativity and vitality to build a happy, enjoyable life. Feeling free widens our perspectives, keeps our minds open, and creates optimism and positivity to engage in a happy life.

"LET ME ASSERT MY FIRM BELIEF THAT THE ONLY THING WE HAVE TO FEAR IS... FEAR ITSELF NAMELESS, UNREASONING, UNJUSTIFIED TERROR,"

—Franklin D. Roosevelt, First Inaugural Address

The purpose of this affirmation was to create a mood and mindset to think and act fearlessly. From personal experience, I strongly recommend that you read biographies of icons and heroes to develop some grit and courage in your mind. Specifically, I highly recommend reading Patrick Henry's speech, "Give me liberty or give me death..." He gave this speech to convince the delegates at the Virginia Convention to send their troops to the war of independence. Time and time again, Americans have been fiercely independent people, and their declaration of freedom glows in their hearts and spirits eternally.

Read about Susan Anthony and Jane Adams, who struggled for decades for equal rights for women. Martin Luther King, Jr. challenged racial discrimination and segregation and led the Civil Rights Movement. He galvanized not only people of color, but also thousands of fair-minded Caucasians to march shoulder to shoulder in Montgomery, Alabama. Dr. King and his followers became a beacon of hope for freedom in America as well as to the civil rights movements across the world.

Explore other influencers of the world. The German philosopher Karl Marx championed the 'workers' right to assert their political power from the bourgeoisie. Likewise, the Russian October Revolution, the Chinese Communist Revolution, the Vietnam Anti-Imperialist War, and Indian Independence struggle roused the masses to fight fearlessly for freedom and independence. Consequently, throughout history, common people gained freedom, and the working classes gained political power, improved their wages, and received better working conditions as well as a fair, equal share in society.

All freedoms—political, economic, social, spiritual, or religious—go hand in hand. People are fully happy when they enjoy total emotional, psychological, and political freedom, which is the purpose of using the affirmation, "live free and fearless." It serves as a reminder to seize your happiness and opportunities.

I want you to know that happiness is the freedom to think and act while doing the things you love in life. Living your dream is happiness. Feeling proficient, self-sufficient, self-efficient, and confident is happiness. Feeling good about things you do, for yourself or others, is happiness. Taking or giving help, gratitude, love, empathy, support, or encouragement is happiness.

Building happiness in your life doesn't require any special efforts— only changing how you think and what you do moving forward. You can work on embedding principles within yourself that can give you a free and fearless feeling. This journey is a self-transformational one for life.

When you worry, fear, or doubt or feel tired, weak, or gloomy, saying this affirmation a couple of times, clear and loud, lifts your spirits. When I practice this affirmation, I mind-map heroes, explorers, scientists, adventurers, and freedom fighters who made sacrifices to achieve modern freedoms. Internally, it helps me orient myself with mental courage and grit.

Fear of the Unknown

David Cunningham was a 55-year-old Caucasian male patient who visited my practice for a routine colonoscopy during the summer of 1997. David worked in Chicago in a manufacturing plant and earned comfortable financial freedom before retiring in Florida. He worried about colon cancer and virtually any cancer in his body.

He scheduled periodic colonoscopies, always pleading to set up the next colonoscopy before it was due because of his fears. He was worried, fearing many things in life. David was scared of meeting new people—particularly women. He feared dating women, much less becoming engaged or marrying.

When I asked why, David said, "I'm a happy man. But I'm imprisoned by my fears." This state of being limited his relationships. He saw psychologists and psychiatrists without any help. Interestingly enough, David carried an eternal smile on his face, despite the worries continuously on his mind.

I counseled David during office visits. He would leave the office pumped up and happy, only to return to the office—even before his next appointment—for another dose of reassurance and encouragement. While David understood he had nothing to fear, he continued to worry. He had a classic case of fear of the unknown.

David set goals to get rid of the fear; he wrote and practiced affirmations to live free and fearless. As he worked towards accomplishing his goals, David came to understand the purpose of life as presented in this book. He was community oriented and charitable, and he often discussed with me the subject of caring for himself and helping his neighbors. I continued to see David until I retired in 2015. He was very much concerned about my leaving the practice; I assured him he would be well cared for by my able associates.

David practiced affirmations and made positive efforts to achieve his goal of being free and fearless. He attended my seminars, workshops, and read my newspaper articles. He continued to find some medical excuse to see me more often than he was supposed to. Each time he visited my office, David asked the same questions, and I would reassure him that he would feel better. Then, he would leave with happiness in his heart.

David depended on my positive encouragement to reboot his mood and fearless mindset. He did very well with continued care for nearly 30 years. He was happy for weeks, and then he returned. As David gave in to his fears long before retirement and continued giving in to them, he never came out of that state of fear fully well. From my experience with him and others, it's essential to work towards releasing fear as soon as possible. Once fear has a hold on you, the longer it goes unaddressed and the harder it is to break from the cycle of worry.

Releasing Fear

Fear is a strong negative emotion. Fear floods the body with harmful chemicals, shifts focus on the feared target, narrows ideas, and can paralyze the body and mind in extreme cases. Frequent morbid or overwhelming fears are disabling and paralyzing; the accompanying chemical load is harmful to the immune system and body functions.

Mild fears in the form of anxiety and worry are defensive, protective, and could be a survival instinct. They served a great purpose in the early stages of human evolution, in the jungles of Africa where our ancestors fought or fled mortal predators in the wilderness. Therefore, it is impossible to eliminate fear, but we can learn to rein it in as soon as it sets off the alarm bells.

People fear many things—heights, water, flying, closed spaces, canyons, and even happiness, success, and change in circumstances. You must question your fears. Where do they come from? Tear them down to pieces with reason, logic, and questioning. Examine how they originated. Ask why, how, and what you're afraid of. Challenge them by asking "What if ?" questions regarding each of them. Play them out in your mind through good, bad, and worse case scenarios—and layout escape routes if necessary.

The fear of the unknown crumbles like a house of cards when you expose it to reason and logic. Exercise courage, conviction, and conscience while thinking about your fears. Building a business, an enterprise, or working on a project can boost your courage to fight back the fear. Most irrational fears can be overcome with applied reason and logic. This rational questioning and bringing self-awareness is called consciousization (bringing our thoughts and behavior back to conscious awareness).

Crude fear in the modern world is an emotional vestige like the appendix of the body. Fear in its family of emotions, such as anxiety, worry, concern, and caution, is a necessary mind body response to prepare, prevent, and protect from impending harm. Fear, real or perceived, can escalate into an emotional rage or phobias. Left unchecked, it becomes an attitude and habit. People often fear and worry, "What if something happens?" Once fear becomes a habit, it's challenging to get rid of it. Fear frustrates, confuses, and complicates the ability to make rational decisions. Morbid fears and phobias need professional counseling to cure.

Self-control can influence your chances of overcoming fear favorably, but don't be a control freak. We cannot control what happens 100%, but we can change the variables significantly in our favor. We live in a rich world with abundant chances. You'll get your chance if you keep yourself open for reaching out and grabbing new opportunities instead of worrying about lost opportunities. Life, from birth to death, is a chance occurrence from an evolutionary perspective—just as it was for the birth of the universe. Only one among the million sperm effects fertilization of an egg in pregnancy and every sperm has an equal chance. Likewise, our opportunities, challenges, successes, failures, and even happiness are a chance occurrence.

Overall, chance prefers the one who is prepared. We, being the intelligent species, have learned to influence those chances in our favor. So, the measure of success or failure, victory or defeat, fame and glory are a chance occurrence to any given time and space. People who know how to play with their chances right will gain the most. Victors are the chance finders, and their victory is itself a chance.

People should be prepared to deal with unexpected events, emergencies, and accidents—including health and finances as well as in personal and professional settings. We should be proactive instead of panicking at unanticipated events. Prepare and plan to take on surprises with contingencies in places, such as troubleshooting and risk management plans, with built-in redundancies and cross covering to deal with unanticipated events. People who don't plan for emergencies suffer the most from the unexpected. Therefore, you should expect the unexpected and make plans to deal with it.

Incompetence, doubt, and guilt can further instill fears; you can defeat these quietly by developing competence and regaining self-esteem and confidence. I call on my conscience during the toughest challenges in life. I can recollect an incidence where my conscience alone comforted and held my spirits while I was at my peak of medical practice. One of my patients wrote to the Florida Medical Board, claiming that I touched her breast inappropriately. My office manager handed me the letter with tears in her eyes. I was shocked when I read it. I couldn't recollect the patient's name or the incidence.

The office manager and I stood silent for a moment after I read the letter. My head was reeling with a lot of questions and the consequences of such complaints. I could lose my license, reputation, and livelihood. My office manager asked, "What now?" I replied, "I have a clear conscience. Let come what may; we will be fine." I consoled her, "This case comes down to my word against the patients, and it's all about the truth."

The investigator found no wrongdoing on my behalf. It took a year of uncertainty and worry on my part as I battled thinking what if the investigator believed the patient's story, but my conscience alone held my spirits up. The final frontier of self-confidence and grit helped me squire off with many challenges in life. The facts will always prevail in the end.

Consciousize Your Fears

Fear is a conditioned habit of your emotional memories. It is a steady and furious subconscious emotion, often taking its grip without you knowing it. Consciousizing is understanding why and what is causing the fear. Finding the cause is where the remedy begins.

As explained in Stage 5, the consciousization technique works to bring subconscious behaviors, habits, and attitudes to conscious awareness, which means we get to know what we do, why we do it, and whether we approve it or not. Consciousization is breaking down an automated habit into its components—why, where, and when—a conscious thought. In other words, we question our subconscious behaviors and treat them with reason and logic.

The lowermost part of our brain, the cerebellum, is the microprocessor of fear. It coordinates all neurological circuitry instantaneously, including the information from our primary emotional controller, the amygdala, and launches the fear response subconsciously. The only way to cure fear is to bring it to conscious awareness (consciousization), and there are many strategies to do so—as shared throughout this book.

In terms of doing this work for yourself, I encourage you to keep a journal of your fears for a month or even six weeks. In great detail, write about every fearful event or thought. Keep track of when, where, and what provokes your fears. Be specific regarding situations and locations. Likewise, note how long it lasted and how it subsided.

By analyzing the data for up to six weeks, you will figure what, why, and how your fears unleash. The locations, situations, and circumstances of the origin of fear can give clues to the underlying causes of fear. A friend of mine breaks out in cold sweats in fear when police cars ride behind him; this fear sprang from a past incidence when police stopped him for disorderly conduct. You will get to know the patterns, factors, or axiomatic thoughts that provoke fear. Once you have all of this information in mind, then you can dispel fears.

Curiosity in a Cycle of Worry

I am a curious person, and curiosity has become my trademark over the years. I want to know and experience what I don't know. I never lost the farmer's mindset of my childhood. I developed resilience and strength through my experiences during childhood and school and while pursuing my career. Whatever help I could find along the way would dry up quickly, and the whole cycle of worrying and looking for funding usually began again, until I would find somebody to bail me out of my predicament. Over the years, my fears hardened and transformed into me believing that help will always arrive somehow from somewhere—in hindsight, that continued to be the case.

At age 11, farming was simple but hard work for me. I worked just as hard as my brother and father in the field. There were days during a monsoon when I transplanted paddy seedling all day in the soaking rain. Farming taught me lifelong patience, resilience, and endurance. Indeed, the rest of my life was a cakewalk for me.

My financial insecurity dissipated once I started an internship. From that point, I never looked back at money as a source of fear. I went to England in the cold winter of 1976. The Western lifestyle and outlook offered me more freedom to think, read, and reflect on past peoples and societies. I was making more money, enjoying comfort, and acquiring more knowledge in the Western world. On that note, I will always believe that experience is power.

In 1980, I moved to the United States, the land of the free and the home of the brave. Upon my arrival, I embarked on my journey towards the American dream—making money and striving for success, liberty, and the pursuit of happiness. I very much enjoyed the American brand of freedom and individuality during my medical practice over the years.

Curiosity remains my social trade. I love learning anything, anywhere, at any time. Google is my best buddy now. I use it whenever I want to know the why's, how's, where's, and when's, etc. I'm curious about people and their attitudes, habits, and behaviors as well as lands, philosophies, qualities, and cultures. Curiosity drove me to go to college when I had no money. The feeling dragged me across the world in migration to other continents, to live, love, and learn. I traveled the world extensively and paid attention to the details of all the locations and peoples I visited. I gained much from understanding how and why people behave.

Curiosity is the mother of learning and helped me to garner knowledge and wisdom. I developed an independent perspective regarding every facet of life and living. I often challenged people to ask me whatever questions they had about life and living. They sometimes did not agree with the answer, which was their choice. My curiosity seeks knowledge, and that's the source of my freedom and fearlessness.

When I think about my demise, it doesn't worry me. Indeed, I see my exit as a random act, but I can improve the chance of my survival if I act smartly. Recently, a friend of mine sent me a story called "die with an empty mind." The moral of the story is to squeeze all the juice out of your life before your demise. Do everything on your bucket list, amend the estranged relationships, and pass away with peace of mind so that you have nothing to fear about reaching the end of life. My mother was well contented with her demise. She often said that she had finished her mission and had nothing else to offer society; she was prepared to leave the planet contended and peacefully.

In my 50s, during my divorce, I realized many of my attitudes and behaviors were modeled after my parents, family, teachers, peers, and society. Therefore, I reoriented my views and values to the new me. I gained the belief that all conflicts among people are related to either natural selection or human-made factors. Therefore, I moved forward with the principle that people should treat others as their cousins, regardless of their color, race, or socioeconomic status. That's my firm belief that gives me peace of mind and a quiet sense of social responsibility.

Living in a fast-changing world, I need to refresh my behavior to fit the current reality. The desire to become and be me was transformational; it is what we call self-realization. I can tell you that once you self-realize, you then become your boss— thinking, being, and acting independently.

Today, I'm a happy man. I keep an empty mind if I'm not doing anything. I simplify things and deal with them efficiently. I keep a clean conscience. I own my mistakes, and I do not feel guilty or suffer from them. I live stress-less and effortlessly. I embrace life's challenges by staying ahead of the curve and taking proactive, preventive steps. I don't let anything bug me. Most choices we make in our life are relative, and I do not sweat too much about finding a perfect choice. After experiencing my happiness, my long-term goal is to help others do the same.

Activity: Consciousization Journal

Yet again, I wholeheartedly recommend keeping a journal of all the issues you face. Continue keeping details regarding any problem you face and review it at a later time. As you do, you will gain greater conscious insight into your subconscious. This activity surely has helped me immensely throughout my life.

Once you know what is explicitly bothering you or causing further issues, you can then use the consciousizing technique to bring your subconscious attitudes, habits, and behaviors back to reexamine them with reason and logic in the prefrontal cortex. This consciousizing is an intense mental force. It supports you towards acting conscientiously and doing things just as you choose, not acting on conditioned behaviors. Of course, I also recommend accepting help from psychologists or even psychiatrists to cure any mortal, long term fears.

Consciousizing Fears, Frustrations, and Problems

Journal the problem for 4 to 6 weeks: categorize the problem: emotional, financial, or psychological. For each of the problems below, note (a) the nature of the problem, (b) the what, where, and when it happened (c) mild, moderate, or severe, and (d) aggravating and relieving factors. When you analyze the data for 4 to 6 weeks for each of the problems, you will begin to understand the causes and cures of each of problem.

Emotional Problem 1: _____

Emotional Problem 2: _____

Financial Problem 1: _____

Financial Problem 2: _____

Psychological Problem 1: _____

Psychological Problem 2: _____

Now that we've gone through building happiness in your life, we can move forward together in our Vehicle of Joy. As all of us commit to charity and supporting one another along the ride, the vehicle evolves into what I like to call, "The Happy Bandwagon." I hope we can work together as we embrace a positive future and live free and fearless.

Conclusion

I hope reading this book convinces you that the modern world offers every opportunity to build a happy life. Contrary to some opinions, all nations are working relentlessly to make this world a better place—along with international agencies such as the United Nations, World Bank, IMF, public charities, private foundations, and many others. They're eradicating disease, illiteracy, hunger, and homelessness while attempting to protect the environment.

The world progress is self-evident if you visit the rural areas of developing countries. I hope you can ignore the surface noise you hear from the media and the press, for they are motivated to report and portray only the worst in the world to grab public attention in order to top ratings and profits. Still, they are capable of doing good work in exposing the socioeconomic ills and evils in society to render a better world for the future.

While you see a lot of turbulence on the surface, I see a different picture beneath the surface. I see a calm, sturdy, and robust subsurface current of human progress sweeping across the globe, which is happening because human survival and progress depend on it. Please, rest assured: the building of a better world for the future is on track. We often can't see it because it is impossible to observe with the naked eye.

The human "invisible hand" organizes social progress, much like the invisible hand that Adam Smith, the Scottish economist, described in his book, *The Theory of Moral Sentiments.* The quality of human activity that each of us indulges in to protect and propagate humanity remains invisible until it reaches a critical mass, then it manifests visibly. Every change, process, and system in the human domain (including the stock market) works the same way. Microcosmic quantitative changes unknown to the human mind and unseen by the human eye become apparent only when it reaches a critical mass and force. This process is much like how our subconscious runs our lives; we know very few things before we take action or speak. We dwell in our conscious mind while our subconscious controls 90% of everything else. The consciousization I recommend in this book is all about making inroads in liberating ourselves from the stranglehold of our subconscious attitudes and behaviors.

My book presents resources and tools grounded in the comprehensive understanding of evolutionary, historical, psychological, and socio-political perspectives of humanity. Utilizing the guidelines and tools I've shared, I am confident you can create a positive life to your liking. If you read this book several times, I imagine you'll more so appreciate on garnish the benefits. I'll be forever grateful if people can use it to improve their lives. The five stages of Chapters 4-8 present the layers of building a Vehicle of Joy, and you can work on each of them separately, simultaneously, or in any order you'd like.

The Happy Bandwagon

As you implement what I've shared in this book, don't waste time or money wandering from pillar to post, frantically making your way to different paths of happiness. This way of life only causes further stress. The concepts I've shared will calm your mind, improve your focus and immune system, relieve your stress, make you feel good, and help you live happily, which was the case for me as I implemented them into my life.

Through practice, I hope you can fly over the zone of stress in life by using these tools. Keep in mind that your emotions and happiness will always be subject to the fluctuations of daily life, but that's the beauty of life. Happiness has no power without its counterpart. Indeed, it feels much more precious and fresher following the bitter aftertaste of sadness. My point is that it's okay to feel fearful, stressed, and sad at the right occasions for a limited time. However, happiness is all about how soon and how well you get back on your happy bandwagon.

I want you to know that you can choose what you love to do, gain any skill you wish, work anywhere you'd like, and live with anybody you wish. What are you waiting for? This village is global, and you're a world citizen. If you can warm up to the world and are willing to explore opportunities, your fears and anxieties will vanish and disappear. Softening my stance and rationality made it easier for me to accept others as they are and respect their feelings and rationale. In and of itself, this acceptance brought me peace and tranquility. My fears, stresses, and frustrations drained in half just by the change of that understanding.

The happiness I am talking about is the same happiness you are all thinking about:

- Regaining peace and tranquility promptly from worries and fears
- Doing things with a clear conscience and full knowledge
- Living free and fearless
- Enjoying and entertaining life

I will say that happiness isn't a one-way road. As you make your way forward in the Vehicle of Joy, you must observe the traffic rules along the bends, turns, ups, and downs. Happiness is learning to drive smoothly and safely staying in the moment. Obviously, happiness is not a suffering-driven life.

Enlightenment Bites

Nothing great ever happens easily or quickly. The Berlin Wall wasn't broken in one day; it cracked for years. At that, it wasn't the wall that broke anyway; it was the will of the people tired of living separately. It was one race, one language, one culture, the kith and kin, families and friends that broke the iron curtain.

Simply starting with the first stage of my book can bring such power to your will. I believe the fun truly lies in doing the tough things first. As Brian Tracey says, eating the frog first will make everything else much easier. This approach to any process sweetens life. As you work the five stages, enlightenment will begin biting you right back.

Everyone in the world wants to become prosperous, to live long and secure, and to lead a happy life. Many of us want to save money for our future and hand over a big estate, heritage, or legacy to our descendants. I get it. Passing on the family estate can help the immediate families for a couple of generations, but building a better world is a greater gift for the generations to come. We are the direct beneficiaries of such generational gifts—the most prosperous, healthy, safest modern world. And, I believe helping others in need will build a better world for future generations, which fulfills the wholesome purpose of humanity. I hope you take full advantage of this book to garnish the basic principles and skills for your benefit.

Reading and understanding, or just knowing, are not good enough until you put it to practice or to work. For example, doctors, healthcare workers, dietitians, etc., know that obesity is bad for health— causing disability, disease, and death—yet, their knowledge is not strong enough of a motivation for them to lose weight. That's the gap between knowing what to do and not doing. We must bridge that gap. Making a choice, committing to action, and sticking with it are a necessity to succeed in any adventure.

I urge you to choose to act here and now. Break the inertia and procrastination. I'm not asking you to spend your time, money, go to gurus, or make a life commitment. I'm asking you to adapt (adopt) the principles and skills I recommend in this book to reorient your outlook and simplify/clarify your actions—and to understand the purpose and function of your work. Implementing these simple principles will save you time and spare your resources, giving you more leisure to relax and enjoy life.

As you practice these concepts, you'll stand tall, strong, balanced, and peaceful—unyielding to outside noise. You'll gain mastery control over your life. You'll know what and why you do from the inside out. Your confusion, frustration, and fears will dissipate for good. Practicing self-affirmations affirms your mindset, elevates your mode, spiritualizes your purpose in life, enlightens your actions, and lastly, causes you to live free and fearless.

An Eternal Gift to Humanity

If you have any questions, clarifications, or comments that you wish to make, please write to me: officialawarenessusa@gmail.com. Also, I recommend that you go to my website: Awarenessusa.org and comment.

In farewell, I wish you the best as you build your happy life. I hope you receive many benefits from my experiences. When you learn something new, I urge you to share it with others. That's your eternal gift to humanity.

The content in this book may seem simple to you when you read it for the first time, but it is deep- rooted in science, evolution, psychology, sociology, and political science. The book wraps social development in its pure subsurface stream at the bottom of the ocean. As said before, I believe it's worth several reads.

I wish you all the best with reading and practicing. The content may not entirely appeal to you, and some of it may seem trite, such as talking about goals. I swear to you, each and everything within these pages is a very important component of building happiness. Thank you so much for investing your time and energy as well as for putting some of the principles into practice.

About the Author

Purnachander R. Bikkasani, MD was born and raised in a small village in the interior part of Southeast India. He was the youngest of seven children in a poor peasant family. By the time he was in fifth grade, his parents had pulled him out of school to work on a farm full time.

Purnachander had many lucky chances and several hands in making him who he is today. A brother put him back in school, a relative lent tuition so he could be enrolled in college, and a roommate guided him to study, which helped him raise his grades from the bottom to the top of the class. While he originally would have been a Veterinarian, he instead became a Doctor of Medicine.

As a medical graduate from Osmania University, Hyderabad, India, Purnachander moved to England to obtain another degree, M.R.C.P. (U.K.), and then migrated to the USA to specialize in Gastroenterology. Following this transition, he built a group practice in Crystal River, Florida, which remained successful for the next 30 years.

In his community, Purnachander ran stress reduction seminars and wrote articles for local and regional newspapers for several years in the '90s. Upon his retirement from medical practice in 2015, he soon founded two nonprofit trusts to help economically, academically, and socially disadvantaged students. His trusts, Awareness USA in America and Chaitanya Saradhi in India, remain his focus as he continues to enjoy his happy life.

Book Description

The book *Joy of Life* authenticates the idea that happiness is a buildable emotion in the modern era. The world produces enough goods and services to meet basic needs and beyond for all citizens. To build an enjoyable, happy life, the author recommends setting up goals and affirmations, learning to deal with conflict and change, committing to charity, and connecting to purpose in life.

This book discusses what real joy is and how to garnish it through daily activities, adapting to adversity, and taking advantage of a genetic set-point of happiness. If you are like the majority of people who suffer and struggle in life—financially, emotionally, or psychologically—I hope to show you how to get over pain and suffering. If you are already doing well in life, the tools and habits presented here will fuel your success and happiness to greater heights.

Made in the USA
Coppell, TX
26 January 2021